GREG LAURIE

with Larry Libby

HOUSE
—OF—
DAVID

A Devotional

30 DAYS WITH THE MAN AFTER GOD'S OWN HEART

FOREWORD BY JON ERWIN

DAVID C COOK

transforming lives together

HOUSE OF DAVID
Published by David C Cook
4050 Lee Vance Drive
Colorado Springs, CO 80918 U.S.A.

Integrity Music Limited, a Division of David C Cook
Brighton, East Sussex BN1 2RE, England

Library of Congress Control Number 2024942963
ISBN 978-0-8307-8882-8
eISBN 978-0-8307-8883-5

The Team: Michael Covington, Stephanie Bennett, Jeff Gerke, Judy Gillispie,
Karissa Silvers, Jason Jones, James Hershberger, Susan Murdock
Cover design: Brian Mellema
Cover photography © 2025 Amazon Content Services LLC

Printed in the United States of America
First Edition 2025

1 2 3 4 5 6 7 8 9 10

120924

To my friend Jon Erwin:

Thanks for telling my life story and the story of the last great spiritual awakening, the Jesus Movement, in the film Jesus Revolution.

Thank you for envisioning this new series on the life of Israel's greatest king—David—and introducing him to a whole new generation that has only at best heard his name in passing.

Thank you for your vision to bring the highest-quality cinematic expressions of the the greatest stories ever told found in the pages of Scripture.

May God bless you mightily in the years to come.

— CONTENTS —

— FOREWORD —

Life is made up of defining moments. I'm a filmmaker and storyteller by trade, so one defining moment for me, as for any filmmaker, is when I was given my first camera. It was an XL-2, and my dad bought it for me with money he didn't have. I was sixteen years old, and to this day it's the best gift I've ever received.

Two days after I unboxed the camera, we flew to Israel to make a documentary called *In the Steps of Jesus*. The Bible sprang to life for me for the first time. I could feel the history. I could see the stories. We stayed in the old city of Jerusalem and visited the tomb of David. It wasn't just the historical significance that struck me but the profound sense of connection to this character who embodied the original "hero's journey"—a warrior poet, a king, and an underdog; a man of profound contradictions, extraordinary accomplishments, and extraordinary mistakes. In the end, he was called a man after God's own heart.

The themes of the story instantly came alive: a young shepherd defeats a giant, becomes the second and most famous king of Israel, unites a kingdom, and pens songs that still echo centuries later. His story, full of great victories and personal struggles, deeply inspired me. For the last two decades, while making films like *American Underdog* and *Jesus Revolution*, I've dreamed of bringing his story to life.

Another defining moment in my life occurred on a beach in California called Pirates Cove. Barely five months after the theatrical release of *Jesus Revolution*, a true story based on a *Time* magazine cover article, I watched my friend and spiritual mentor, Pastor Greg Laurie, stand in the same waters he had fifty years before and baptize more than forty-five hundred new believers as another twenty thousand stood on the beach with me. We witnessed life imitating art in the same way that art had imitated life.

Most people were there because they had seen the movie and wanted to experience it for themselves. They wanted to live out an iconic scene in the film where people were baptized, which we filmed to closely match the iconic photography from the article. In that moment, standing on the beach, I saw with my own eyes the true purpose of my work: to inspire hope and restore faith in things worth believing in.

Pastor Greg is truly one of my favorite people. I'm deeply inspired by his teaching and writing. After fifty years of obedience in ministry, Pastor Greg has undoubtedly taught the life of David more than anyone, so I was excited to learn that he wanted to create a devotional inspired by the series *House of David*. Reading through this book made me feel like a biblical archeologist as he uncovers profound insights into these ancient texts, illuminating not just the psalms of David, written three thousand years ago, but also the spirit in which they were written—a spirit of unwavering faith amid life's trials. If David was a man after God's own heart, then Greg's devotional made me understand the heart of David.

David's psalms are profoundly personal prayers of lament, songs of praise, and declarations of trust from David to his God, each echoing the struggles and triumphs we all face. Somehow, Greg's ability to unpack these themes with clarity and compassion makes this book not just a study of Scripture but a guide for navigating our own spiritual journeys.

I think we are drawn to David's story because we all yearn for a "hero's journey" of our own. We all want to step into our destiny. We all want to play a role in a grand design beyond ourselves. So I hope that as you read this devotional and watch our series, you'll be inspired to choose a life of adventure instead of ease and step into a calling beyond yourself, just like David did when he slew the giant.

In these pages, written through decades of study and teaching, you will find not just commentary but an invitation to engage with the sacred text on a personal level, encouraging you to bring your own heart's cries to the Lord in the personal way David did. Thank you, Greg, for sharing your insights and for leading us into this deeper exploration. May this book be a beacon of hope and a catalyst for spiritual growth for all who read it.

Jon Erwin

— INTRODUCTION —

Welcome to *House of David*, my friend.

The devotions in this book are thoughts I've had over the years about Israel's greatest king. They are adapted from my many sermons about this man after God's own heart. I hope you will love remembering his life and reading his beautiful and often anguished words and seeing how he always ended up in adoration of the Lord.

I am so thrilled that my friend Jon Erwin (who wrote and directed the film *Jesus Revolution*, which is about my wife, Cathe, and me) is directing a new cinematic series for Prime Video on the life of this amazing man, King David. Jon was able to make this happen through a new independent studio called Wonder Project.

I believe *House of David* will be a game-changer series that will introduce a whole new audience—numbering in the millions—to this paradoxical and powerful leader of the nation of Israel.

As I walked through the incredible sets for this series, including the palace of Saul and the boyhood home of David, I felt as though I had gone back in time.

The book you are holding is my own way of connecting you to the life and writings of David. I hope you will see that there is so much for us all to learn from him today.

David was a true believer. He loved the Lord with all his heart. And even after he sinned, he always turned back to the Lord again—which is what we should do as well. David experienced it all, from the highest highs to the lowest lows. He came from total obscurity, but his fame skyrocketed. A song written about him was such a hit that it even got some airtime in Philistia.

He was a shepherd, an outcast, a warrior, a musician, and a poet, and he became the greatest king Israel ever had.

But even more important than that, he was part of the most exclusive genealogy in all the world—the genealogy of Jesus.

Think of it! When Jesus walked this earth, He identified Himself as the Son of David. He could have said He was the son of Abraham or the son of Judah or even the son of Adam. But He chose to be identified with the youngest son of Jesse, as imperfect as David was. Jesus was referred to by this title sixteen times in the Gospels. When the blind beggar Bartimaeus heard that the Lord was passing by on the road to Jericho, he didn't yell, "Jesus of Nazareth, have mercy on me." No, he cried out to the Son of David, and the Son of David responded. (See Mark 10:46–52.)

David, however, was not only a shepherd, a warrior, and a great king, but he was also an adulterer, a murderer, and a liar. The Bible makes no attempt to airbrush his biography. We see him at the heights, and we hear his broken voice from the depths. But even in his brokenness and sorrow, he ministers to us. He brought us the blessing of Psalms 32 and 51, where he cries out to God for forgiveness and begs Him not to take away His Holy Spirit or withdraw His presence.

As we look at David's story, we see the real message. It's not really about the greatness of David. It's about the greatness and grace and kindness of God, who gave David a second chance to serve Him.

When I think of the house of David, one poignant story comes to mind.

After all the trials of his fugitive years, when David was firmly settled on the throne of Israel, he had a deep desire to build a temple for the Lord. He told Nathan the prophet, "Look,... I am living in a beautiful cedar palace, but the Ark of God is out there in a tent!" (2 Sam. 7:2).

David wanted to show his love and loyalty to God by building a house for Him. But it wasn't to be. Through Nathan, God told David, "Are you the one to build a house for me to live in? I have never lived in a house.... I have always moved from one place to another with a tent and a Tabernacle as my dwelling" (2 Sam. 7:5–6).

So it was a no, but a gentle no. And then something very tender happened. The Lord said in effect to David, "It won't be your job to build Me a house, but I am going to build *you* a house."

The Lord explained, "Furthermore, the LORD declares that he will make a house for you—a dynasty of kings! For when you die and are buried with your ancestors, I will raise up one of your descendants, your own offspring, and I will make his kingdom strong. He is the one who will build a house—a temple—for my name" (2 Sam. 7:11–13).

I love what happened next. David went to the Lord's tent and "sat before the LORD." Overwhelmed, he said, "Who am I, O Sovereign LORD, and what is my family, that you have brought me this far?" (2 Sam. 7:18).

It was the grace and kindness of God that established the house of David. And it is the same undeserved, unmerited favor that has established my house—and yours, if you belong to Him.

Someday in Heaven, I look forward to meeting David. I'm betting he has written quite a few new songs since he left the planet. But much more than that, I want to go for a walk with the Son of David.

And that will be best of all.

THE LORD IS MY SHEPHERD

Because the Lord is my Shepherd, I have everything I need!
Psalm 23:1 (TLB)

Inspired by Psalm 23

We're all living in a crazy, chaotic world right now.

Someone might say, "Yes, but so did our parents, their parents, and *their* parents."

It's true of course. There has always been enough heartache and turmoil to go around on our fallen planet. Sadly, pandemics, toxic politics, and strife have been around from earth's earliest days.

Even so ... I can't help feeling that as the time draws near for our Lord's return, the very foundations of our world are being shaken as never before. Even if you're not a news junkie, you can't avoid feeling an unusual tension in the air. War around the globe, unprecedented violence in our streets, and totally insane, unexpected tears in our social fabric that our grandparents could have never imagined in their wildest nightmares. All this is fueled by digital news and social media—with a device in nearly everyone's hand.

We need some calm in the midst of the storm. We need an oasis in the desert. We need a safe place to retreat to, and I'm not talking about Martha's Vineyard or Cabo San Lucas. Actually, no matter where we live, we can find the refuge we crave in the book of Psalms.

And for many of us, Psalm 23 is the crown jewel. Charles Spurgeon called it the "pearl of psalms." The great British preacher went on to say, "It has charmed more griefs to rest than all the philosophy of the world.... It has sung courage to the army of the disappointed."[1]

Next to the Lord's Prayer, this is probably the best-known passage in all of the Bible—and also the best loved. This particular text has brought hope to millions, possibly billions, of people over the years. It has been read by pastors and chaplains to people in hospital beds and even to people on their deathbeds. For some, these are the final words they hear as they pass into eternity.

And they are very, very good words.

Every believer ought to commit Psalm 23 to memory. I memorized it in the King James Version many years ago, but any translation works well.

Speaking of memorization, I heard about a Sunday school teacher who told her class, "I want you all to memorize Psalm 23, and next week I'm going to have you each recite it." As the next week went on, one little boy was really struggling with it. All too soon the following Sunday arrived, and it was his turn to stand in front of the class.

He said, "The Lord is my shepherd." He paused, then said, "And that's all I need to know." And he sat down.

Well, there's some truth there. If you truly know the Lord as your shepherd, everything changes. This relationship will be the single most determining factor through all the years you walk on earth, no matter where you are or what happens in your life.

When we hear the word *shepherd*, we might imagine an idyllic scene, painted in soft pastels. There the shepherd is in the green grass among the wildflowers and butterflies, staff in hand, keeping watch over his flock of fluffy, cotton-white sheep. Maybe the sun is setting in the background.

But a shepherd in David's day was not a prop in a pretty picture. In some ways, a shepherd was a warrior as well as a protector and a provider.

Whatever you may be dealing with in your life right now, whatever problems and dilemmas and impossible situations you woke up with this morning, remember this: *The almighty Creator of the universe is your shepherd.*

Let that sink in a moment.

When David wrote the words of Psalm 8, he was probably out with his flock at night, looking up at the stars. (And can you imagine what the heavens looked like before there was a single electric light in the whole world?) He wrote:

> When I look up into the night skies and see the work of your fingers—the moon and the stars you have made—I cannot understand how you can bother with mere puny man, to pay any attention to him! (vv. 3–4 TLB).

But God does pay attention. He pays very close attention to every detail of your life.

I love how David said, "The Lord is *my* shepherd." He could have said, "The Lord is *a* shepherd," and that would've been true. The Lord is indeed a shepherd, but David personalized it and said, "The LORD is *my* shepherd; I shall not want" (Ps. 23:1 NKJV).

Read these next words as if you were seeing them for the first time: *God is interested in you as an individual. He has a plan for your life.* I love the passage in Jeremiah where God says, "I know the thoughts that I think toward you,... thoughts of peace and not of evil, to give you a future and a hope" (Jer. 29:11 NKJV).

God could have said, "I know the thoughts I think toward humanity." But He didn't. He made it personal. He said, "I know the thoughts I think toward *you*."

Do you know that God thinks about you? Have you ever let that concept really sink in? God cares about you. David himself wrote: "The LORD directs the steps of the godly. He delights in every detail of their lives" (Ps. 37:23).

The Lord is your shepherd.

I love how Paul personalized the death of Jesus when he wrote: "I live by faith in the Son of God, who loved me and gave Himself for me" (Gal. 2:20 NKJV).

Yes, it's true that Christ died for the whole world. Jesus said it best in John 3:16: "For this is how God loved the world: He gave his one and only Son." But again, Paul brings that truth home when he says, "He loved *me* and gave Himself for *me*."

So remember this: When others forget you, God is there as your shepherd. David wrote later in Psalm 27:10, "Even if my father and mother abandon me, the LORD will hold me close." As a matter of fact, David's dad, Jesse, didn't even acknowledge him when the prophet

Samuel showed up to meet the family. In one version of 1 Samuel 16, Jesse refers to David as "the runt ... out tending the sheep" (v. 11 MSG).

But David knew that even if his family disregarded and overlooked him, he had a personal Shepherd who never would.

As the patriarch Jacob was dying in a land far from home, he reflected back on his life and made this statement about the Lord: Jacob called Him "the God who has been my shepherd all my life, to this very day, the Angel who has redeemed me from all harm" and "the Mighty One of Jacob,... the Shepherd, the Rock of Israel" (Gen. 48:15–16; 49:24).

That is what He wants to be for you. He wants to be your shepherd through all of life, to this very day.

I can't think of anything in this world better than that.

A PAGE TORN FROM DAVID'S JOURNAL

The LORD is my shepherd, I lack nothing.
    He makes me lie down in green pastures,
he leads me beside quiet waters,
    he refreshes my soul.
He guides me along the right paths
    for his name's sake.
Even though I walk
    through the darkest valley,
I will fear no evil,
    for you are with me;
your rod and your staff,
    they comfort me.

You prepare a table before me
  in the presence of my enemies.
You anoint my head with oil;
  my cup overflows.
Surely your goodness and love will follow me
  all the days of my life,
and I will dwell in the house of the LORD
  forever.

                                        (Ps. 23 NIV)

Shepherd and Protector

*Even when I walk
through the darkest valley,
I will not be afraid,
for you are close beside me.
Your rod and your staff
protect and comfort me.*

Psalm 23:4

Inspired by Psalms 23 and 91

God is our shepherd, and we are His sheep.

By the way, that's not much of a compliment. I know sheep are cute little creatures, but they are honestly among the dumbest animals on the face of the earth. Now, if the Lord would have said, "You are My dolphins," that might have been pretty cool. Dolphins are very intelligent. Scientists have determined that dolphins can actually evaluate their surroundings and figure out solutions. Researchers say they can also show complex emotions.[1]

He might have even said, "You are My dogs." Well, that's okay. Most people love dogs. After all, dogs can be very intelligent and brave, and they make great companions.

Even cats are more intelligent than sheep. They have survival skills. Cats have an incredible homing instinct, allowing them to use navigational tools like star patterns, the angle of the sun, and even the earth's magnetic field.[2] There have been instances of cats finding their way home from as far as eighty miles away.

Good luck trying that with sheep. They can't even find their way to a watering hole. (Remember Psalm 23:2? "He makes me lie down in green pastures, he leads me beside quiet waters" [NIV].)

You've heard the expression that cats have nine lives? Not sheep. Sheep can't even defend themselves. They can't bite, and they can't run. They're basically leg of lamb in the making. They might as well carry mint jelly around with them and say, "Hey, you hungry? Kill me. And this will make me taste even better."

One writer put it this way:

> Sheep are dumb and directionless. They are also *defenseless*. Left to themselves, sheep will not and cannot last very long. Just about any other domesticated animal can be returned to the wild and will stand a fighting chance of survival. But not sheep. Put a sheep in the wild and you've just given nature a snack.[3]

The Bible says, "All we like sheep have gone astray; we have turned, every one, to his own way" (Isa. 53:6 NKJV). I read that in Turkey a single sheep calmly walked off a cliff. That's not the smartest thing to do, but a sheep might do that. The animal just walked off a cliff for no particular reason and fell to its death. But here's what is crazier: At least fifteen hundred other sheep followed him. They all walked off the cliff.[4]

That sounds really stupid—but maybe just a little bit familiar? Are we ever affected by peer pressure? Do we ever find ourselves doing things we wouldn't normally do because other people do them and say we should do them as well?

Sheep need help. I mean, *lots* of help. And so do we. We need the help and protection of God. We need the step-by-step wisdom of His Word. We need the calm, guiding voice of the Holy Spirit. Without those things? Well, just look around you. Check out the evening news.

We're lost.

So that's the way it is; we who follow Him are His very own sheep. And by the way, He actually loves to take care of us. He loves being our shepherd. Jesus said, "So don't be afraid, little flock. For it gives your Father great happiness to give you the Kingdom" (Luke 12:32 TLB).

Sheep are completely dependent on their shepherd, just as you and I are completely dependent on our Good Shepherd.

David also was a good shepherd.

When this young man volunteered to fight Goliath in the Valley of Elah, he gave his credentials as to why he thought he could bring that freakish giant of a man down. He explained to King Saul:

> I have been taking care of my father's sheep and
> goats…. When a lion or a bear comes to steal a lamb
> from the flock, I go after it with a club and rescue

> the lamb from its mouth. If the animal turns on me,
> I catch it by the jaw and club it to death. I have done
> this to both lions and bears, and I'll do it to this
> pagan Philistine, too, for he has defied the armies of
> the living God! (1 Sam. 17:34–36)

That's pretty hardcore. He sounds like a ninja out there defending his animals. (How many lions have you grabbed by the jaw recently?)

The son of Jesse could really wield a club, but he was also pretty handy with a sling and a stone.

People who calculate such things have said that a person who is adept with a sling can get that rock flying 100 to 150 miles per hour. Like a guided missile. The Bible tells us that the stone David flung at Goliath *sank into* the giant's forehead. It didn't bounce or ricochet off his hard head; it penetrated like a musket ball. The hulking Philistine never saw it coming. One moment he was laughing and sneering at the upstart shepherd running to meet him, and the next moment it was lights out.

Since October 7, 2023, when twelve hundred innocent Israeli civilians were senselessly slaughtered by Hamas, a terrorist organization fueled by Iran, continued attacks and missiles have been fired at the Jewish state.

But Israel's defense is also strong. One of their defensive systems is called the Iron Dome, but another rocket defense system they use to protect their nation is called David's Sling.

I find that moving. After more than three thousand years, the people of Israel still remember their greatest king as a defender and protector. And that is true of our great shepherd and king as well. The Lord is your protector.

In Psalm 91, the psalmist underlines this wonderful truth:

> This I declare about the LORD:
> He alone is my refuge, my place of safety;
>   he is my God, and I trust him.
> For he will rescue you from every trap
>   and protect you from deadly disease.
> He will cover you with his feathers.
>   He will shelter you with his wings.
>   His faithful promises are your armor and
>   protection.
> Do not be afraid of the terrors of the night,
>   nor the arrow that flies in the day.
> Do not dread the disease that stalks in darkness,
>   nor the disaster that strikes at midday. (vv. 2–6)

I love how both day and night are covered.

When I first open my eyes in the morning, the Lord is my protector. I can put my life into His hands. When my head hits the pillow at night, the Lord is my defender and shield. So whatever you are facing right now, remember this: *The almighty Creator of the universe is your shepherd.*

Does that mean nothing unpleasant will ever happen to me? Not at all. Even Stephen, one of the Lord's choicest servants, died by stoning outside the city gates (see Acts 7). It wasn't a pleasant way to die. But I don't think this young man would have traded that moment for anything. As he was dying, he "gazed steadily into heaven and saw the glory of God, and he saw Jesus standing in the place of honor at God's right hand. And he told them, 'Look, I see the heavens opened and the Son of Man standing in the place of honor at God's right hand!'" (vv. 55–56). What an entrance! His Shepherd was saying, "Come on Home with Me, Stephen. No one will lay a hand on you again."

David went *mano a mano* with bears and lions to defend his flock. Just a kid with a club, a sling, and a courageous heart. And how many attacks of the Enemy—with an evil army bent on our destruction—has our Shepherd defended us from? Perhaps in the last twenty-four hours? How many times has He shielded us from the fiery arrows flying at us out of darkness and the predators prowling in the night?

We won't know the answers to those questions until we are safely on the other side with Him. But in the meantime, the apostle Paul gives us this assurance: "The Lord is faithful; he will strengthen you and guard you from the evil one" (2 Thess. 3:3).

You can take that to the bank.

A Page Torn from David's Journal

This I declare about the LORD:
He alone is my refuge, my place of safety;
   he is my God, and I trust him.
For he will rescue you from every trap
   and protect you from deadly disease.
He will cover you with his feathers.
   He will shelter you with his wings.
   His faithful promises are your armor and
     protection.

(Ps. 91:2–4)

—— DAY 3 ——

PROVIDER AND GUIDE

You serve me a six-course dinner
right in front of my enemies....
My cup brims with blessing.
Psalm 23:5 (MSG)

Inspired by Psalms 23 and 25

Our Shepherd is our provider.

The very first verse of Psalm 23 says, "The LORD is my shepherd; I have all that I need."

As we've already noted, sheep are basically helpless. They need the provision of a shepherd. And isn't that true of us as well?

Someone might say, "I see your point, Greg. But no, not in my case. Actually, I'm very successful, and I've made a lot of money. It's come about through my shrewd investment strategies and my hard work (not to mention my deep humility)."

Well, perhaps you have done that. You've done well. I've known people with the gifting to be great entrepreneurs and shrewd investors, and they do work very hard. And, surrendered to Christ, they can be great assets to the kingdom of God around the world.

But where does that ability come from? Here's a clue: It doesn't come from Stanford, Harvard, the Wharton School of Business, or the Fox Business channel.

It comes from God.

Scripture leaves no room for doubt. Deuteronomy 8:18 says this: "Remember the LORD your God, for it is he who gives you power to get wealth" (ESV). The apostle Paul was a little bit more pointed: "What do you have that God hasn't given you? And if everything you have is from God, why boast as though it were not a gift?" (1 Cor. 4:7).

If you've achieved wealth, it's a gift from His hand. If you have found success in any endeavor, it's by His enablement. Everything you have is a gift from God. Your wealth. Your job. Your family. The beat of your heart. Your next breath.

Life itself is a gift beyond expression. Tragically, many people don't realize this until it's almost gone.

One day, unless Jesus comes for us first, we will come to the end of our journey. We will take our last step. Say our last words. Breathe our last breath. In that moment, in that instant between earth and Heaven, between time and eternity, you will remember—with incalculable joy—"The LORD is my shepherd; I shall not want" (Ps. 23:1 NKJV). And you will also say, "I will dwell in the house of the LORD forever" (v. 6 NKJV).

Make the Lord your shepherd. That's the very best way to live in this life, and that's the secret of contentment. Paul writes in Philippians 4:11–13:

> Not that I was ever in need, for I have learned how
> to be content with whatever I have. I know how

to live on almost nothing or with everything. I have learned the secret of living in every situation, whether it is with a full stomach or empty, with plenty or little. For I can do everything through Christ, who gives me strength.

Contentment should be the hallmark of the godly person. And make no mistake: Contentment in life does not come from what you have. *It comes from knowing Christ.* Hebrews 13:5 says, "Keep your lives free from the love of money and be content with what you have, because God has said, 'Never will I leave you; never will I forsake you'" (NIV).

Our Shepherd is also our guide. David wrote, "Even when I walk through the darkest valley, I will not be afraid, for you are close beside me" (Ps. 23:4).

Are you in a valley right now, as you read these words? By "valley," of course, I mean a season of difficulty, hardship, or sorrow. You might feel overwhelmed by some unexpected circumstances that have crowded into your life. Maybe it almost seems as though God Himself has abandoned you.

David was certainly no stranger to calamity and hardship. He lived a hard life. He was rejected by his father, who didn't even think of him when asked to introduce all his sons to Samuel. Then, when he was anointed to be king, David met with immediate opposition from King Saul, who made it his life's mission to kill David.

For the next *fifteen years*, David became a fugitive with a price on his head. He was never safe. He could never let his guard down. Even after David finally became king, his own son turned against him and tried to kill him. And once again the son of Jesse had to go into the wilderness, hunted like a wild animal. David knew all about valleys.

You might say, "You know what? I don't like valleys. Lord, I don't do valleys. I'm a mountaintop person. I want the sun shining. I want the sky blue. I want the birds singing. I don't want to go through that valley." And God effectively says to us, "You want to reach that next mountaintop? You have to go through this valley first. That's the way to the mountaintop."

In fact, fruit doesn't grow on mountaintops; it grows in valleys. And by "fruit," I mean spiritual fruit. Some of the most important lessons you'll learn as a Christian will not come through the so-called good times. They'll come through the hard times. The dry times. Right in the middle of the most horrendous trials we can imagine, the patriarch Job made this statement: "But he knows the way that I take; when he has tried me, I shall come out as gold" (Job 23:10 ESV).

I love what David says: "Even when I walk through the darkest valley, I will not be afraid, for you are close beside me" (Ps. 23:4). He didn't say, "Even when I collapse in the darkest valley," or "Even when I crawl through the darkest valley."

David said, "I'm *walking through* this with my Shepherd. I'm going to keep walking, and I'm not going to give up."

That's my word of encouragement to you. You will get through this valley, whatever it may be. So keep walking with your Shepherd. That was what kept David going through all those lean, grueling years on the run. He wasn't alone. He had the best companion anyone could have in life or beyond life.

And so do you.

One evening as the shadows fell, Jesus suddenly said to His disciples, "Let's cross to the other side of the lake" (Mark 4:35). So they all piled in the boat and started out. And that's when trouble hit. Mark records the scene like this:

> Soon a fierce storm came up. High waves were breaking into the boat, and it began to fill with water.
>
> Jesus was sleeping at the back of the boat with his head on a cushion. The disciples woke him up, shouting, "Teacher, don't you care that we're going to drown?"
>
> When Jesus woke up, he rebuked the wind and said to the waves, "Silence! Be still!" Suddenly the wind stopped, and there was a great calm. (4:37–39)

What if Jesus had said before the storm hit, "Let's go to the middle of the Sea of Galilee and drown together, shall we?" Who would have boarded that boat? But He didn't say that. He said, "Let's go to the other side," which meant they would certainly arrive at their destination.

He didn't promise them a first-class passage or an easy journey, but He did promise them a safe arrival. It's the same with us. Our Shepherd will get us through the storm, through the heartbreak, and through the narrow canyons.

Valleys don't last forever, but His love does. The Shepherd will certainly get us to the other side.

He said so.

A Page Torn from David's Journal

Show me the right path, O LORD;
   point out the road for me to follow.
Lead me by your truth and teach me,
   for you are the God who saves me.
   All day long I put my hope in you....

The LORD is good and does what is right;
   he shows the proper path to those who go astray.
He leads the humble in doing right,
   teaching them his way.
   The LORD leads with unfailing love and
      faithfulness.

(Ps. 25:4–5, 8–10)

THE FIRST STEP

Show me the way I should go,
for to you I entrust my life.
Psalm 143:8 (NIV)

Inspired by 1 Samuel 16; Psalm 25

When a man of Samuel's reputation and stature would show up in some city or town in Israel, it was a big deal.

The old prophet cast a very long shadow. If he walked through the gates of Jerusalem, that would be one thing. But if he suddenly showed up in a little village like Bethlehem, that was another matter entirely.

Bethlehem was like Podunk, USA. There wasn't much there. It was just one of the hundreds of little towns and villages in the land. Nothing ever happened in Bethlehem. The only reason most of us today know about Bethlehem at all is because that is where Christ was born. And why was He born in Bethlehem? Because He was the root and offspring of David.

Centuries after Samuel, God, speaking through the prophet Micah, said:

But you, Bethlehem Ephrathah,
Though you are little among the thousands of
        Judah,
Yet out of you shall come forth to Me
The One to be Ruler in Israel,
Whose goings forth are from of old,
From everlasting. (5:2 NKJV)

When the prophet Samuel unexpectedly strode into town, people must have freaked out a little. Samuel had been the supreme judge and spiritual leader of Israel longer than anyone could remember. Saul may have been king at the time and head of state, but Samuel had a mantle of divine authority that went deeper still.

So when people looked out their windows and saw the prophet on Main Street—probably the most recognizable figure in the whole country—it was just a little intimidating for the elders of Bethlehem. Scripture says that "when he arrived ... the elders of the town came trembling to meet him. 'What's wrong?' they asked. 'Do you come in peace?'" (1 Sam. 16:4).

In effect they were saying, "Is everything cool, sir? Have we done something? Are you coming here to call judgment down on us?" But Samuel said something like, "No, it's all good. I want to offer a sacrifice to the Lord, so let's have everybody gather together for the occasion—and by the way, make sure Jesse and his sons show up."

God had told Samuel that he was supposed to anoint one of Jesse's sons as the future king of Israel. But who was Jesse? Which one of his sons did the Lord mean? And what would happen then?

This is what I find interesting: God didn't tell his prophet who the next king would be—not so much as a hint. He only told him, "Go to Bethlehem, and check out the house of Jesse."

This is yet another reminder to all of us that God leads us one step at a time.

As I look back on my own life, after fifty years in the ministry, I wish I could tell you I had it all planned—that everything happened just as I predicted and imagined it would. But nothing could be further from the truth.

After I came to Jesus, I just took one step at a time. I started by cleaning toilets and pushing a broom around Calvary Chapel Costa Mesa. Then I took the next step, and the next, and the next. It was a day at a time. I didn't have anything close to a blueprint to follow. All I knew was that I wanted to follow Jesus and needed to be obedient to the next thing He would ask me to do. If you saw the *Jesus Revolution* film, you already know this.

I'm reminded of the story of Philip in the book of Acts. He had been having a powerful ministry up in Samaria. People were coming to Christ, and the power of God had been present in a big way, with miracle after miracle among the people. The evil spirits in the area were so disturbed that they came out of people with screams and took off for parts unknown (see 8:7).

The Samaritan Crusade was an ongoing success. And then, seemingly out of the blue, we read this: "As for Philip, an angel of the Lord said to him, 'Go south down the desert road that runs from Jerusalem to Gaza.' So he started out" (vv. 26–27).

Leave Samaria? Walk away from a huge opportunity? To go *where*? The Lord didn't give him any details. He didn't tell him who he should speak to or what he might expect. The angel had simply said, "Head south on the Gaza Highway." And to his credit, Philip obeyed.

When Philip finally arrived on that desert road, he saw the man he was to speak to—a visiting dignitary from Ethiopia, riding along in his chariot and reading from the book of Isaiah. Okay, but what was Philip supposed to do? The Holy Spirit gave him the next step: "Go over and walk along beside the carriage" (v. 29).

It comes down to this: God's way *becomes* plain when we start walking in it. Obedience to revealed truth guarantees guidance in matters unrevealed.

So here is what I recommend to people seeking God's will for a given day—or for the rest of their lives. Just start where you are. Be obedient to the last thing God told you to do, and keep your eyes and ears open to God's Spirit.

Start with the Word of God. Begin by reading your Bible every day. (There's a no-brainer.) And here's another step: Have a prayer life. Call out to the Lord and take time in quiet moments to listen for His voice. If you feel confused or perplexed, tell Him about it. These are disciplines we all should maintain.

Start with the obvious. Take that first step, and God will show you what to do next.

Back in Bethlehem at the sacrifice, Samuel asked to see the sons of Jesse, and the old sheep rancher was happy to comply. He paraded seven strong sons in front of the prophet, and they were all great specimens of Hebrew manhood. These were healthy, strong, strapping young men—especially Eliab, who stood out among the others. Do you remember the classic old Western *The Magnificent Seven*?

Well, here they were in little Bethlehem, walking slowly in front of Samuel for his perusal.

And step by step, as each son took his brief walk in front of the prophet, the Lord whispered in Samuel's ear: "Not that one. And no, not that one either. No, that's not the one." On it went until all the sons had passed by.

We pick up the story in Scripture:

> Then Samuel asked, "Are these all the sons you have?"
>
> "There is still the youngest," Jesse replied. "But he's out in the fields watching the sheep and goats."
>
> "Send for him at once," Samuel said. "We will not sit down to eat until he arrives."
>
> So Jesse sent for him. He was dark and handsome, with beautiful eyes.
>
> And the LORD said, "This is the one; anoint him." (1 Sam. 16:11–12)

So the old prophet pulled out a skin of oil and anointed David as the future king, before the shocked and unbelieving eyes of his father and seven brothers.

Notice that the Lord had Samuel check out all of Jesse's boys—all seven of them—before they brought the right one in.

That's the way it is in our lives sometimes. It's step by step. Day by day. Obedience by obedience. Until that last day when our next step is right out of this world and into His presence.

A Page Torn from David's Journal

Teach me your ways, O LORD;
  make them known to me.
Teach me to live according to your truth,
  for you are my God, who saves me.
  I always trust in you....

Because the LORD is righteous and good,
  he teaches sinners the path they should follow.
He leads the humble in the right way,
  and teaches them his will.
With faithfulness and love he leads
  all who keep his covenant and obey his
      commands.

Keep your promise, LORD, and forgive my sins,
  for they are many.
Those who have reverence for the LORD
  will learn from him the path they should follow.

(Ps. 25:4–5, 8–12 GNT)

THE LORD SEES THE HEART

Men and women look at the face; GOD looks into the heart.
1 Samuel 16:7 (MSG)

Inspired by 1 Samuel 16; Psalm 139

The Lord had given His prophet Samuel a set of very specific instructions about locating the next king of Israel to replace Saul:

> "Fill your flask with olive oil and go to Bethlehem.
> Find a man named Jesse who lives there, for I have
> selected one of his sons to be my king....
>
> Take a heifer with you ... and say that you have
> come to make a sacrifice to the LORD. Invite Jesse
> to the sacrifice, and I will show you which of his
> sons to anoint for me."
>
> So Samuel did as the LORD instructed. (1 Sam.
> 16:1–4)

It was a little like a divine navigation program. *Load up a heifer* (read: big cow). *Merge onto the highway. Take the Bethlehem exit. Meet the townspeople at the town square. Make sure Jesse's family shows up. Then wait for further instructions.*

Samuel followed along, trying to make all the right turns. But when the sheep rancher Jesse and his boys arrived at the ceremony, the prophet got out over his skis. Jesse proudly paraded seven of his sons before the visiting prophet. And the very first guy to walk the runway looked like a sure winner.

Samuel took one look at Eliab, the eldest, and thought to himself, *Now it all makes sense. This guy looks every inch a king—he's strong, tall, good-looking, confident. A touch of gray around the temples. He looks like he came from Central Casting. I can just picture a crown on his head. In a few seconds, the Lord will say to me, "That's the one! Anoint him."*

But it didn't happen that way. The Lord interrupted Samuel's speculations with these clear words: "Don't judge by his appearance or height, for I have rejected him. The LORD doesn't see things the way you see them. People judge by outward appearance, but the LORD looks at the heart" (1 Sam. 16:7).

It's true, isn't it? Whether we admit it or not, we really do judge by outward appearance. We size a person up. We take their measure. We pigeonhole men and women—almost instantly—based on a whole litany of criteria. And most of what we conclude we would never say out loud. *Probably an old hippie ... She's had some work done ... Man bun ... Strange tattoos ... Boomer ... A little too slick ... Weight problem ... Gen Z ... Clothes don't match ... Seems insincere.*

And on and on we go. We actually make decisions about people we don't know at all. We classify them and draw conclusions about them before we have even spoken to them. And when it comes to ourselves, most of us are really concerned about how we look and how we appear to others. Think about your last selfie with the family. You might have heard yourself say, "Oh, don't post that one. That's a weird expression. My smile looks plastic. I need to hold in my stomach. Take another one."

We want to look good. That's why we use filters and special effects before we post a picture of ourselves. We focus so much on the outside, just as Samuel did. And just as He did with Samuel, the Lord has to take us to task sometimes for our superficial judgments.

God looks on the inside. Seventeenth-century pastor and poet George Herbert wrote that God "sees hearts, as we see faces."[1] The psalmist said, "He knows the secrets of every heart" (Ps. 44:21).

Could you imagine what it would be like if you and I had this ability—if we could actually see a person's heart and really know what they were thinking? I'm not sure that would be a good thing. I think I might be disappointed a lot. Someone would come up to me after church and say, "Great sermon, Pastor. Loved it." But inside they're thinking, "That was a dud. Big waste of time."

Jesus knew human hearts all too well during His time on earth. And He wasn't shy about calling people out! He would say to the Pharisees, "You guys look so holy on the outside, with your flowing robes and little boxes of Scripture on your foreheads. But inside you're like a graveyard full of bones and corruption." (See Matt. 23:5, 25–28.)

How did He know that? He knew it because He was and is God, and God looks on the heart. God knows what's happening on the inside. He knows every crevice of our souls.

In our culture today, we place so much emphasis on the way we look. Americans spend upward of sixteen billion dollars a year on cosmetic surgery. All that money spent on trying to appear to be something we're not.[2] (But what if some of that emphasis was placed on *who we are*—in our hearts and souls?)

Back in 1960, when then-Senator John F. Kennedy had his debate with Vice President Richard Nixon on TV, a huge audience was watching. Nixon did not look his best, with perspiration appearing on his lip and a bit of a five o'clock shadow. Quite a contrast to the tanned, telegenic Kennedy.

Funny thing: Those who watched the debate on TV felt that Kennedy won.[3] But those who listened to the debate on the radio felt Nixon was the winner.

It was all about outward appearance.

Never make evaluations of someone based on appearance alone.

Yet we do make decisions based on the attractiveness of a man or woman. You might say we are hardwired that way. Studies have shown that even *newborns* are drawn to an attractive face.[4]

But God looks past all that. He sees the character traits that everyone else overlooks. He sees the longings and humility and hunger for God that no one else perceives. Remember how He deliberately stopped at a well outside the town of Sychar and waited for a certain Samaritan woman to come with her bucket to draw water?

Who else in the whole world knew or cared that this woman had a thirst for God—a thirst she had carefully hidden through long years and five indifferent husbands? *Jesus knew.* He read it in her heart. He took note of her desire. And it drew Him to Samaria like a magnet.

He also sees the potential that no one else could predict or imagine.

- He saw in Moses—an elderly backcountry shepherd with a criminal record—the potential to lead a nation out of slavery.
- He saw in Gideon—the timid son of a Baal worshipper from a nondescript clan in Manasseh—a mighty military leader.
- He saw in Ruth—an idol-worshipping Moabite widow—a loyal heart, a loving wife, and a future great-grandmother to Israel's greatest king: David.
- He saw in Esther—a gorgeous young woman who won a beauty contest—one who could become queen and save her people, the Jews.
- He saw in Mary—a common teenage girl from a half-pagan town—the future mother of the Son of God.
- He saw in Simon—a fisherman—the potential to become a great leader and legendary apostle.
- And He sees in you what you will become one day.

Sometimes we look at our lives and wonder why God would choose us. But here's what we need to realize: God doesn't just see us in our weakness; He sees us for what we can become.

We might see a lump of clay; God sees a beautiful vase. We might see a blank canvas; God sees a finished painting. Where we see problems, God sees solutions. Where we see failure, God sees potential. And where we see an end, God sees a new beginning.

From cover to cover, the Bible is full of unlikely, little-noticed, barely qualified people who allowed God to touch them, raise them up, and use them for His glory. He would later remind David:

> I chose you to be the leader of my people Israel when
> you were a mere shepherd, tending your sheep in
> the pastureland. I have been with you wherever you
> have gone and have destroyed your enemies. And I
> will make your name greater yet, so that you will be
> one of the most famous men in the world! (2 Sam.
> 7:8–9 TLB)

He plucked David out of a sheep pasture. No college degree. No sports trophies. No military training. No family connections. No SAT scores. No fancy résumé. None of that.

But what he *did* have was something God saw right away. In fact, He saw it before David was born or even conceived. Samuel prophesied it before he'd ever laid eyes on this young man: "The LORD has sought out a man after his own heart and appointed him ruler of his people" (1 Sam. 13:14 NIV).

David had a heart for God. And that qualified him.

That's a good thing to remember before we draw conclusions, good or bad, about people. It's a good thing to remember before we draw conclusions about ourselves. The apostle Paul said, "Don't cherish exaggerated ideas of yourself or your importance, but try to have a sane estimate of your capabilities by the light of the faith that God has given to you all" (Rom. 12:3 PHILLIPS).

Bottom line: If you put God first in your life, seek Him with all your heart, and humbly depend on Him, He will find you and use you for His glory. It doesn't matter if you're in a sheep pasture, a prison, a rehab center, Hollywood, or Scratch Ankle, Alabama.

He never stops looking for men and women who truly seek Him.

A prophet named Hanani said it best to one of David's descendants: "For the eyes of the Lord search back and forth across the whole earth, looking for people whose hearts are perfect toward him, so that he can show his great power in helping them" (2 Chron. 16:9 TLB).

A PAGE TORN FROM DAVID'S JOURNAL

O LORD, you have examined my heart
   and know everything about me.
You know when I sit down or stand up.
   You know my thoughts even when I'm far away.
You see me when I travel
   and when I rest at home.
   You know everything I do.
You know what I am going to say
   even before I say it, LORD.
You go before me and follow me.
   You place your hand of blessing on my head.
Such knowledge is too wonderful for me,
   too great for me to understand!

(Ps. 139:1–6)

The Shadow of a Giant

When I am afraid, I will put my confidence in you. Yes, I will trust the promises of God.

Psalm 56:3 (TLB)

Inspired by 1 Samuel 17; Psalm 56

Do you have any giants running loose in your life right now?

Chances are, you do.

Most of us have at least one or two—kicking down our fences and stomping brazenly across the middle of our landscape, or lurking just over the horizon, waiting to make their move.

What do I mean by a giant? I'm talking about those seemingly insurmountable problems and issues that life brings our way.

Perhaps it's a giant called *Fear.*

Maybe there's something out there, something dark and sinister prowling around the perimeter of your life in recent days that absolutely terrifies you. Every now and then, you feel its long shadow fall across your day, and fear grips your heart. Or you sense it looming close in the middle of the night, somehow deepening your darkness and robbing you of sleep.

And even though it retreats a little sometimes, stepping into the background, it never completely goes away.

Or maybe it's a giant of *Personal Sin*. You have an area in your life that continually defeats you, keeps you in bondage, and steals your joy. No matter what you do, no matter how you've prayed, no matter what you've tried, you just can't seem to defeat this thing.

Sometimes you think you've pushed it away or forced it into submission. A few days go by. Maybe even a few weeks. Sometimes you will even get through a whole month and begin to breathe a sigh of relief. And just that quickly, it comes roaring back with a vengeance, wreaking havoc as though it had never been away. You hear its taunting laugh, a laugh that shakes the windows of your soul, and you wonder, *Am I ever going to be free from this?*

It might be a giant named *Addiction*—one of the ugliest, most evil giants you could ever face. You've been trying to break free from it for months. Even years. Or decades. And this intruder in your life has been mocking you and defeating you day after day. You've fought and you've battled, you've wept and you've pleaded, but it only seems to loom larger with the passing of time.

There are all kinds of giants skulking around out there, with names like *Pride, Envy, Gossip, Greed, Gluttony*, and *Lust*. In some cases, it's as though they have taken up residence in your life and made themselves at home. And in your heart, you've almost come to the conclusion that you'll have to live with that gross giant the rest of your life.

Sometimes the giant is some heavy, pressing issue you're facing. Something you can't seem to find an answer for or get resolved. Maybe it's a spouse who doesn't know the Lord. And as the years go by, they don't seem to be any closer to coming to faith. In fact, in some ways they seem further off than ever. Maybe it's a prodigal son or daughter. You've been praying for this child to come back to the Lord, but there has been no response, no hopeful signs, no turning. In fact, it may even seem like they are getting worse. And you wonder, how am I ever going to overcome this? Will this giant ever go away?

So how do you deal with a giant, anyway?

It's a handy thing to know. It's good information to stick in your back pocket in case you encounter one along your path or feel one shaking your house in the middle of the night.

In young David's life, the first giant he had to face was a big, ugly Philistine named Goliath. The saga unfolds for us in 1 Samuel 17.

What a story! No matter how many times you've heard it or read it, it makes your heart beat a little faster. What a victory this was for David—invigorating all Israel. Like ripples spreading outward from a stone tossed into a still pond, David's faith and courage swept through the whole army, changing them from cringing cowards to the courageous warriors God intended them to be.

And the Philistines? *They* became the cringing cowards, throwing down their weapons and running like scared rabbits. The will and the pride of the enemy had been broken.

Where did it all start? It started with a young man who stepped out of the safety zone and was willing to take a chance and trust God.

What about the giants we face in our own lives right now? As we've already noted, you may have something that looms large and is seemingly undefeatable in your life. After enduring failure after failure, you've come to the place where you believe that giant will just always be there. It will be a big, ugly, humiliating part of your landscape from now on. In that sense, you've come to accept the giant.

That was the problem with the Israelites. Goliath had become a part of their lives. For forty days he had lumbered up to the battle line to shout his challenge and his mockery. The number forty in Scripture is always the number of testing. Twice each day Goliath snarled insults and blasphemy at Israel's finest soldiers. After all those days, they'd gotten used to it. They could set their watch by it.

Maybe that's what has happened with you and your giant. You've started thinking, *This is just a part of my life. I don't want it. I don't like it. But I've gotten used to it. It's always going to be there.*

No! You must be willing to accept that this giant can and, by the grace of God, *will* fall. But it will mean climbing out of that foxhole and stepping out to the battle line to face that thing. It will mean taking a chance and putting your faith in God as never before.

A Page Torn from David's Journal

O God, have mercy on me,
   for people are hounding me.
   My foes attack me all day long.
I am constantly hounded by those who slander me,
   and many are boldly attacking me.
But when I am afraid,
   I will put my trust in you.

I praise God for what he has promised.
  I trust in God, so why should I be afraid?
  What can mere mortals do to me?...

You keep track of all my sorrows.
  You have collected all my tears in your bottle.
  You have recorded each one in your book.

My enemies will retreat when I call to you for help.
  This I know: God is on my side!
I praise God for what he has promised;
  Yes, I praise the LORD for what he has promised.

                              (Ps. 56:1–4, 8–10)

HOW TO HANDLE
A GIANT

My eyes are always on the LORD,
for he rescues me from the traps of my enemies.

Psalm 25:15

Inspired by 1 Samuel 17; Psalm 25

God had been preparing young David for the day when he would face the oversized Philistine Goliath.

David had been a faithful and protective shepherd to his sheep. But shepherds were not passive observers; they also had to be seasoned warriors.

David had fended off bears and lions, even killing a large cat by grabbing its beard and stabbing it. As he made his case as to why he should face the mighty warrior Goliath in the Valley of Elah, David said, "I go after [a predator] with a club and rescue the lamb from its mouth. If the animal turns on me, I catch it by the jaw and club it to death. I have done this to both lions and bears, and I'll do it to this pagan Philistine, too, for he has defied the armies of the living God!" (1 Sam. 17:35–36).

In *House of David* on Prime Video, director Jon Erwin imagines how this may have happened. In his narrative, David's beloved mother, who taught him how to play the lyre, was slain by a certain lion that had haunted the family for a period of time. As a young boy, David had gone over the stone wall surrounding their property against his parents' wishes and put himself in the place of danger.

Seeing that her son is gone, David's mother frantically searches for him and finds him in the lion's gaze with only moments to live. She engages the lion and tells David to run, and she is brutally mauled by the beast and ultimately dies.

David is devastated and feels he bears responsibility for his mother's death. His father, Jesse, also blames David for it.

David makes it his mission to hunt down this ravenous lion. He eventually corners it in its lair and kills it, quoting Scripture to calm his doubts.

So what would he think about going up against a giant man? A struggle, yes, but not an impossibility.

David had arrived at the Israelite battle line just in time to hear Goliath bellow his challenge. He heard the men in Saul's army say, "Have you seen this man who has come up? Surely he has come up to defy Israel" (1 Sam. 17:25 NKJV).

Goliath had "come up." The Hebrew word here means to "ascend" or "climb."

That wasn't good.

At some point in his forty-day intimidation of Israel's army, Goliath had begun actually crossing the ravine at the base of the Valley of Elah and *coming up* on Israel's side, perhaps getting closer each day.

No doubt Goliath had been a bully and an intimidator his whole life. (Can you imagine him as a kid on the playground?) So he wasn't content to simply stand on the Philistine side jeering at Israel with the troops. He wasn't just down in the valley shouting up taunts. He was coming up on their turf, getting in their faces.

Scripture says this had been going on, twice a day *for forty days*.

What do we learn from this? If you tolerate a giant, if you give him room, if you continue to let him speak his piece, he will take over your territory. Before you know it, he'll be right up on your doorstep—and then sleeping in your spare room. And in time he will seek to be the "lord of the manor," demanding your obedience.

If you give a little to the Devil, he's going to want more. That's the way the game works. He will come to you and say, "Just give me *this*. It's a small thing. No big deal. You can have the rest. Just this. That's all. I don't want any more."

So you give in, and almost immediately he comes back and says, "Okay, so I lied. Now I want some more. Why are you surprised? What did you expect? Even Jesus called me the Father of Lies. Now yield me some more. Do it now!"

The truth is, he wants everything. He wants all of you. And if he can't take you to hell, he will at least try to bring hell to you. He will start with a little so he can get a lot. That's why you don't want to give the Devil a foothold in any way, shape, or form. That's why you don't want to run from giants or tolerate their presence for days on end.

In Ephesians 4:27, Paul reminds us: "Do not give the devil a foothold" (NIV).

Another way to say it might be, "Don't leave a half-open door, giving him easy access into your life." Close the door to anger and bitterness and lust and pride, and turn the dead bolt.

So what do you do with a giant?

You don't yell at it or threaten it or pretend to ignore it, like Israel's troops did in the Valley of Elah. No, you *attack*. You run at it and kill it as fast as you can. That's the only way to deal with it. You have to declare war on these things.

Look at 1 Samuel 17:48. "As Goliath moved closer to attack, David quickly ran out to meet him."

I love that. As this colossus lumbered toward him, David was saying, "You want some of this, Highpockets? Let's go." He couldn't wait to get in Goliath's face. The Philistine giant may have expected the much-smaller man to run around in circles and rely on his quickness and ability to dodge here and there. But that's not what happened. David ran right at him, and death was in his hand.

While David ran, he was whipping around that sling of his like a propeller, building up momentum. He'd had lots of practice at it. What else do you do when you're stuck in the wilderness with a bunch of dumb sheep for companions? You pray, play your tunes, and practice with your sling. After endless hours of perfecting his technique, he could probably knock a butterfly off a rock at fifty paces. When lions or bears came out of the woods looking for lamb chops, David could bring them down with a single stone.

So what was Goliath? As far as David was concerned, he was just another big, wild animal running amuck among the sheep.

He let that stone rip like a guided missile, and it sank right into the giant's broad forehead. For the briefest of moments, Goliath was probably stunned. *What happened? What hit me?* And then, like an old-growth pine tree, he came crashing face first into the ground.

You see, David didn't waste time with feints and dodges and fancy footwork. He didn't try to talk his enemy to death. He ran right at that giant and let loose.

We need to do the same with the giants that confront us. Let's say you are facing the giant of pornography. That's a big one for many people these days. It's just so much more accessible today than it has ever been before. There was a time when a person had to go to a seedy theater in the bad part of town to view it. Now it's a mouse click or swipe away. There you sit at your computer with no one around, and the World Wide Web is before you. With just a few simple clicks, you can call up images that no one should ever see.

And like a fly in a spider's web, you are caught.

Once you've been there, once you've given in, once you have left the door open—just a crack—the giant has access to beat you up again and again. I have seen lives and marriages and whole families utterly devastated and destroyed by pornography.

Don't play with it. Don't toy with it. Don't coddle it. Don't tolerate its presence in your life. It is powerful, and it is dangerous, and it is a creation of hell.

You need to attack it straight on.

You need to bring it out into the light of day. It starts when you put aside the pretenses and get honest with someone you trust. You talk about it. Nobody wants to do that, but you *must* do that. You have to attack this giant head-on, or it will grind you to a pulp.

David fought Goliath in the light of day. And that's where we must fight our giants. *Force* the giant out into the light. Stop hiding it. Stop making excuses for it. Stop lying to yourself. Stop pretending it's not there. Recognize it. *It is a giant*, and it is going to destroy you and everyone you love if you don't take your stand.

But remember where you're taking that stand: in the strength of the Lord and the power of His might. And then you are going to defeat that menacing enemy in the power and authority of the King of Kings.

The Devil doesn't want us to know these things. That's not hard to figure out: He wants to keep us trapped. He wants to keep us cowed and intimidated. He wants us to think we're always going to be under the control of this vice or sin or problem.

In our distorted thinking, we somehow end up picturing God as too small and Satan as too large. We need to get things back into their proper perspective and realize that Satan is nowhere near the equal of God.

We need to remember and rely on the fact that Satan is a created being who was soundly defeated at the cross of Calvary. Before His crucifixion on the cross, Jesus said, "Now is the judgment of this world; now the ruler of this world will be cast out" (John 12:31 NKJV). Referring to that same event on Calvary, Jesus said, "The prince of this world now stands condemned" (John 16:11 NIV). Through His death on the cross, Jesus destroyed him who held the power of death. That is the Devil.

So what does all this mean?

Just this: It means you don't fight *for* victory. You fight *from* it.

You don't pray, "O Lord, please give me the victory." Instead, you pray, "Lord, thank You that the victory has been won at the cross of Calvary. I stand on that victory. I stand in the Lord and the power of His might. I've got my armor on now, heavenly Father. You won't give me more than I can handle. And I'm going to attack that giant, and by Your strength I'm going to see that giant come down."

That's what happened for a young, backcountry shepherd named David, and thousands of years later, we get to follow in those footsteps of faith.

A Page Torn from David's Journal

In you, LORD my God,
   I put my trust.

I trust in you;
   do not let me be put to shame,
   nor let my enemies triumph over me.
No one who hopes in you
   will ever be put to shame....

See how numerous are my enemies
   and how fiercely they hate me!

Guard my life and rescue me;
   do not let me be put to shame,
   for I take refuge in you.
May integrity and uprightness protect me,
   because my hope, LORD, is in you.

(Ps. 25:1–3, 19–21 NIV)

Don't Fight Alone

There is a friend who sticks closer than a brother.
Proverbs 18:24 (NIV)

Inspired by 1 Samuel 19, 23

David had no idea of what awaited him in the future after his epic victory over Goliath. If he had known, he might have hired out as a shepherd somewhere far, far away.

Like Egypt. Or Mars.

Maybe he had felt lonely and unfulfilled out there on the backside of obscurity, watching over the family flock. But after he found himself caught up in the gears of national politics, and after Saul had turned on him and begun hunting him like an exhausted fox from one hole to another across the length and breadth of the land, he probably looked back on his shepherding stint as the good ol' days.

Oh, man, those were the days. All I had to deal with were bears and lions and sleeping out in the cold at night. But I had my harp, my poetry, my target practice, and the shining stars, and the Lord was with me. What wonderful days those were.

Killing the Philistine champion led to fame and fortune and popularity for David. But not everyone was a fan.

When the Lord's favor on David's life became obvious, Saul started seeing him as a threat. And that began a long, lean, mean string of fugitive years, staying on guard 24-7 just to save his skin. What killing Goliath had actually done for David was lead him into one of the deepest, longest, darkest valleys of his life.

At this point, David was barely twenty. An overnight hero and celebrity, he became the hottest item in Israel. That kind of instant adulation would have brought down a lot of people right then and there. But David took it all in stride. He handled it all so well.

But he had to face another giant. Goliath was long gone, but now David had to put up with the paranoid, relentless attacks of a jealous King Saul. For years and years to come, David would have no rest, no peace. Saul hunted him day and night. He would promise to stop and then be at it again the very next day.

Knowing David would need a friend to face this new giant, God provided a real blue-chip guy: Prince Jonathan, the son of Saul. Jonathan was the very person to guide David through this strange, heady new environment of royalty, palace politics, and intrigue.

David might easily have been resistant to a friend from this quarter, imagining some sort of conspiracy or plot in the works and not wanting anything to do with Saul or his kin. But the son of Jesse decided to make a friend out of an individual who could have been—maybe should have been—a natural enemy.

Jonathan turned out to be the best friend he would ever have, and their hearts knit together. In this relationship, we learn a little bit about what friendship really ought to be.

A true friend is willing to sacrifice.

You don't have to beg a friend for a favor. You just ask. In fact, your friend might even be upset with you if you *don't* ask. If you had a crisis in your life and chose to keep it from your friend in your hour of need, they might be a little disappointed or irritated with you.

A real friend *wants* to help and doesn't shrink back from commitment. When Prince Jonathan wanted to show David the level of his allegiance, he took the royal robe off his own shoulders and gave it to the former shepherd. He also gave him his armor—including his sword, his bow, and his belt. A true friend is there to assist you no matter what and doesn't keep score.

A true friend will staunchly defend you.

Jonathan spoke well of David before his father, Saul, who had turned on him. In 1 Samuel 19:4–5, Prince Jonathan stood before his dad, the king, and pleaded for his friend. By doing so, he risked both his royal position and his life.

Jonathan had no illusions about what kind of man his father was. He'd seen his dad's temper and instability. It was a risk—even for Saul's own son and heir—to speak up for David. But the young prince was ready to step into the gap for his friend, in spite of the trouble it might cause.

Friends will not betray you.

Friends will not be one person to your face and then another person as soon as you leave the room. If the conversation suddenly turns against you, a false friend will either clam up and say nothing or just go with the flow.

That's a betrayal. And a real friend won't do that. They will speak up for you, even at the risk of getting hammered with anger, scorn, or harsh retribution.

As Oscar Wilde was known for saying, "A true friend always stabs you in the front." I think that's so true. An enemy stabs you in the back, but a friend stabs you in the front. In other words, a friend tells you the truth, to your face. Even when it hurts.

As Proverbs 27:6 says, "Wounds from a sincere friend are better than many kisses from an enemy."

If you have a friend who loves you enough to confront you when you're doing the wrong thing or going the wrong direction, thank God for that person. Sure, it's uncomfortable. For both of you! But conversations like that are incredibly rare and valuable.

Do you have a friend who has been walking along the cliff edge of danger and self-destruction? If you see that peril and say nothing, not wanting to cause a scene or offend them, you're not a true friend at all. If you love someone, you'll risk anger, embarrassment, and even rejection to keep that person from destroying their life and family.

After you have committed the situation to the Lord in prayer, go to that person in humility and love, and say, "I could be off base here, and I could be reading this wrong, but here is what I see. Let me tell you my concern ..."

Prince Jonathan was loyal to David in the midst of intolerable circumstances. From the moment he pledged his friendship to David, he stayed in David's corner. It wasn't easy. It was uncomfortable, heartbreaking, and even dangerous. But he never wavered. He was so true that many years after Jonathan's untimely death, David was still looking for ways to honor him and bless the remnants of his friend's family.

A true friend is an encourager.

When David was down, when life was crumpling around him like a cardboard house in the rain, Jonathan did everything he could to stay in his life and lift him up. The Bible says:

> So David saw that Saul had come out to seek his life. And David was in the Wilderness of Ziph in a forest. Then Jonathan, Saul's son, arose and went to David in the woods and strengthened his hand in God. And he said to him, "Do not fear, for the hand of Saul my father shall not find you. You shall be king over Israel, and I shall be next to you. Even my father Saul knows that." So the two of them made a covenant before the LORD. (1 Sam. 23:15–18 NKJV)

David was heartsick and afraid. No doubt his strong faith in God was being tested at that time as never before. He was in a dark and lonely place, and he felt like all the world had gone against him. But Jonathan searched David out to encourage him. He went to David in the woods. He searched for David in the wilderness, and he kept looking for his friend until he found him.

Are you that kind of friend? If you heard your friend was in some kind of trouble, would you be willing to keep looking for him even if he had changed his address or didn't answer his phone? Would you keep after it even if your friend had found his way into some dark and uncomfortable places?

We like to think of the warm and sunny side of friendship. The times of laughter and conversation and mutual hobbies and shared dreams. But there is another side to genuine friendship, isn't there? And it isn't such a pleasant scene. It means hanging in there with someone who is off on a wrong path, or in trouble, or perhaps terminally ill.

Don't turn away when your friend is facing a giant. Don't leave your friend to walk down into the Valley of Elah alone. Don't avoid the situation because it makes you sad or uncomfortable. Be there for him. Stand by her. Pull your friend out of harm's way, even when it's uncomfortable or risky.

What did Jonathan do when he finally found his fugitive friend in the wilderness? Scripture says he "strengthened his hand in God" (1 Sam. 23:17 NKJV). He was saying, "Hang in there, David. You're God's man. You have destiny written all over you. Hold on to the Lord, trust in Him, and He will deliver you."

When I think of the word *encouragement*, I think about someone who *breathes courage into the heart and life of another*.

Do you have a friend who encourages you? Someone you can call up when you're down? Someone who will seek you out when you find yourself in a dark and lonely place? Someone who will refresh your faith in the Lord when times look bleak?

Thank God for friends like that.

Be a friend like that.

A Page Torn from David's Journal

> David now lived in the wilderness caves in the hill country of Ziph. One day near Horesh he received the news that Saul was on the way to Ziph to search

for him and kill him. Saul hunted him day after day, but the Lord didn't let him find him.

(Prince Jonathan now went to find David; he met him at Horesh and encouraged him in his faith in God.

"Don't be afraid," Jonathan reassured him. "My father will never find you! You are going to be the king of Israel and I will be next to you, as my father is well aware." So the two of them renewed their pact of friendship; and David stayed at Horesh while Jonathan returned home.)

(1 Sam. 23:14–18 TLB)

When the Bottom Drops Out

When I am overwhelmed,
you alone know the way I should turn.

Psalm 142:3

Inspired by 1 Samuel 21; Psalm 142

It was a new low point after years and years of low points.

Exhausted and in fear for his life, David had sought refuge from Saul in a Philistine city with the king of Gath. What a plan! What could possibly go wrong?

In fact, just about everything.

> David escaped from Saul and went to King Achish of Gath. But the officers of Achish were unhappy about his being there. "Isn't this David, the king of the land?" they asked. "Isn't he the one the people honor with dances, singing,

> 'Saul has killed his thousands,
>   and David his ten thousands'?"

David heard these comments and was very afraid of what King Achish of Gath might do to him. So he pretended to be insane, scratching on doors and drooling down his beard.

Finally, King Achish said to his men, "Must you bring me a madman? We already have enough of them around here! Why should I let someone like this be my guest?" (1 Sam. 21:10–15)

So the brave young man who had been promised the kingship of Israel pretended to be insane, slobbered in his beard, and then ran for his life to the wilderness to hide in a cave. I can almost hear Satan whisper in his ear, *Wow, David, you're on a roll, aren't you? You've really covered yourself in glory this time, haven't you?*

How did David feel about that? We don't have to wonder, because he spilled his guts to the Lord in Psalm 142. And here we are, some three thousand years later, on the other side of the planet, and we can read the very words he scrawled in his journal in the back of that cave.

> I cry out to the LORD;
>   I plead for the LORD's mercy.
> I pour out my complaints before him
>   and tell him all my troubles.
> When I am overwhelmed,
>   you alone know the way I should turn.

Wherever I go,
   my enemies have set traps for me.
I look for someone to come and help me,
   but no one gives me a passing thought!
No one will help me;
   no one cares a bit what happens to me. (vv. 1–4)

I love how David shifts gears in the middle of that psalm. It's pretty remarkable when you think about it. Somehow, in the back of the dark and musty hole in the rocks, he steps back from his one-person pity party and gets a fresh perspective. He turns the page in his journal and begins to write again:

Then I pray to you, O LORD.
   I say, "You are my place of refuge.
   You are all I really want in life.
Hear my cry,
   for I am very low.
Rescue me from my persecutors,
   for they are too strong for me.
Bring me out of prison
   so I can thank you.
The godly will crowd around me,
   for you are good to me." (vv. 5–7)

The turning point comes with the words "then I pray" in verse 5. Don't you love how he stops on a dime and changes direction in his prayer? Right in the middle of a deep, heartbroken complaint, with despair pulling him lower and lower, he looks up and says, "You're my last chance, my only hope for life! Oh listen, please listen; I've never been this low" (vv. 5–6 MSG).

So what should you do when the bottom drops out? When your life falls apart like a soggy cracker?

You need to look up. You need to put your focus on God, not on your problems.

You could say the same about the times we're living in.

All around it seems like society is unraveling, crime is increasing, and the family is disintegrating, and it seems that way because it's actually happening before our very eyes.

Add our smartphones to the mix with our constant scrolling, and it only adds gas to the already burning fire. These things that are happening are what the Bible calls "signs of the times" (Matt. 16:3). They are signposts telling us one thing: Jesus is coming again.

So how should we react to all this?

Jesus said, "When these things begin to happen, *look up* and lift up your heads, because your redemption draws near" (Luke 21:28 NKJV).

David needed to look up too.

Yes, David had his troubles, as we all do. He had been falsely accused, betrayed, separated from loved ones, and chased from pillar to post across Israel. Yet here he is, putting his trust in God.

David poured out his complaints to the Lord. One version says, "I spill out all my complaints before him, and spell out my troubles in detail" (Ps. 142:2 MSG). Did you know it's okay to do that? It's truly okay to complain to God in your prayers. He can handle it. He understands.

Some of us think we need to be polite in our prayers or that we should somehow suppress what we are really thinking or feeling. But how crazy is that? He already knows exactly how we feel. David himself realized that when he wrote, "I'm an open book to you; even from a distance, you know what I'm thinking" (Ps. 139:2 MSG).

God actually wants to hear what you are thinking and feeling in your heart of hearts. He wants to hear the things you haven't been able to tell anyone else—and can barely admit to yourself. David himself wrote: "O my people, trust in him at all times. Pour out your heart to him, for God is our refuge" (Ps. 62:8).

It's okay to say to the Lord, "Lord, I don't really like this situation I'm in. I don't like the circumstances that surround me. I don't want this, Lord! Help me!" Yes, it's good to also say, "I want Your will above my own." But in the middle of your situation, it's good to just cry out to Him, to pour out your worries and sorrows into His lap. He *wants* you to!

The Bible tells us to talk to God, "casting all your care upon Him, for He cares for you" (1 Pet. 5:7 NKJV).

The Greek word for "casting" used by Peter is not the normal word for throwing something. Rather, it is a word that signifies a definite act of the will by which we stop worrying about things and let God assume the responsibility for our welfare.

Why should we do this? Peter reminds us: "for He cares for you."

The word *cares* means God is mindful of your interests. If it's a concern to you, it's also a concern for Him.

It's like taking out the trash. I don't know how it works in your home, but I am the one responsible for taking our trash cans out to be emptied each week. For some reason, I will procrastinate doing it. It's not really a hard task, because my trash cans have handles and wheels, but I still put it off.

We do the same with our burdens and worries. We put off casting them on God.

I have some advice for you: It's time to take out the trash.

When the Israelites criticized and turned against Moses, he "cried out to the LORD for help" (Ex. 15:25). When godly King Hezekiah received a letter threatening his life, "he went up to the LORD's Temple and spread it out before the LORD" (Isa. 37:14). In essence he said, "Look at this, Lord! This is outrageous! What are You going to do about this?"

I love that. How long has it been since you took all your worries and fears and doubts and anxieties and just spread them out in the presence of the Lord? Maybe your life feels like a jigsaw puzzle that someone has just dumped from the box onto a table. Nothing seems to go together or make sense. Tell Him so! Ask Him to put the pieces together, and He will hear your prayer (as He has for me ten thousand times over).

When news reached John the Baptist's disciples that their leader and friend had been beheaded by King Herod, they risked their own lives to retrieve and bury his body. Then they went and told Jesus (Matt. 14:12). It was exactly the right thing to do. When your heart is broken and your plans have splintered, you don't get alone and go into a depression. You don't turn to alcohol or drugs. You go and tell Jesus about it, realizing that He wants to hear and that He has all the time in the world to listen to every detail.

Even Jesus Himself cried out to His Father in the garden of Gethsemane. The Bible says that He "fell face downward on the ground, and prayed, 'My Father! If it is possible, let this cup be taken away from me. But I want your will, not mine'" (Matt. 26:39 TLB).

May I loosely paraphrase those words? He's saying, in effect, "Father, I really don't want to do this. Everything in Me shrinks from this. If there is any other way, please show Me."

But there was no other way. And Jesus accepted the most bitter cup that anyone has ever received, and He drank it to the bottom. Even on the cross, at the worst moment of all, He cried out the words "*Eli, Eli, lema sabachthani?'* (which means 'My God, my God, why have you forsaken me?')" (Matt. 27:46 NIV). But again, He cries out *to* God—not *against* God.

When the bottom drops out, you need to cast your cares on God. What do you do when your family or friends abandon you? What do you do when you're betrayed? What do you do when a health crisis casts a shadow over your family? What do you do when your very life is threatened?

You do what David did in the spooky depths of that cave: You call out to God and cast your cares on Him. You say with David, "You are my place of refuge. You are all I really want in life. Hear my cry, for I am very low."

And the God of all comfort hears your cry. Every time.

A PAGE TORN FROM DAVID'S JOURNAL

How I plead with God, how I implore his mercy, pouring out my troubles before him. For I am over- whelmed and desperate, and you alone know which way I ought to turn to miss the traps my enemies have set for me. (There's one—just over there to the right!) No one gives me a passing thought. No one will help me; no one cares a bit what happens to me. Then I prayed to Jehovah. "Lord," I pled, "you are my only place of refuge. Only you can keep me safe.

"Hear my cry, for I am very low. Rescue me from my persecutors, for they are too strong for me. Bring me out of prison so that I can thank you. The godly will rejoice with me for all your help."

(Ps. 142 TLB)

WALKING THE WALK

Test me, LORD, and try me,
examine my heart and my mind;
for I have always been mindful of your unfailing love
and have lived in reliance on your faithfulness.

Psalm 26:2–3 (NIV)

Inspired by Psalm 1

A few nights ago, my granddaughter Stella invited me to her Saturday night Bible study for teens. The ages range from eighteen all the way down to eleven.

She said, "Papa"—that's what they call me—"would you come over to the Bible study? It'll freak the kids out." I thought to myself, *That's an offer I can't refuse! What a great thing for a bunch of kids to do on a Saturday night.*

So I showed up, and the whole crew was there, ready to dig into the Word. I said, "Why don't I talk to you about Psalm 1?" and they immediately opened their Bibles. I'd been preparing a message on that psalm, and to me, it seemed to be all about the choices we make in life.

"You guys are young," I said, "and have your whole lives in front of you. What you may not realize is that the choices you make *today* will shape and impact the rest of your life. It's the same for us older people too. We need to choose well to experience God's very best."

And looking out at those young, intent faces, I found myself longing for God's best in every one of their lives.

We went through Psalm 1 and, point by point, I showed them how it applied to their lives—young as they were—and to all our lives.

It comes down to a pretty simple question. Do you want to be a happy person? If you want to be a happy (blessed) man or woman, boy or girl, do the things the psalmist says in the six verses of Psalm 1—and don't do the things we're told not to do.

It's the very first psalm in our Bibles, but did David write it? No one knows for sure. If he did, he apparently didn't sign it. While many of the psalms begin with the line "A psalm of David," this one doesn't. Some have spotted similarities to the writings of David's son, Solomon, in the book of Proverbs.

In any case, David lived the reality of these words and found great favor and blessing in his life. How much favor? Just think of it: To this very day, the blue and white Star of David flag waves on a million flagpoles—in Israel and around the world.

Psalm 1 is a study in contrast. It shows us that life is filled with cause and effect. You do *this*, and *that* will happen. You do *that*, and *this* will happen. We need to think very carefully about our choices. And I'm not just talking about the big ones, like, *Where should I live? Should I go to college? Who should I marry?* I'm talking about the everyday decisions that may very well change the whole course of life.

Boiling down the psalm to its essence, it says: The happy person walks the right way. Psalm 1:1 states:

> Blessed is the man
> Who walks not in the counsel of the ungodly,
> Nor stands in the path of sinners,
> Nor sits in the seat of the scornful. (NKJV)

Walking is a big deal in Scripture. It's an activity that speaks of cadence and consistency. It's not a spectacular thing to do, but it's a very good analogy of the Christian life. On more than one occasion, the Bible compares our relationship with Jesus to a walk.

> As you received Christ Jesus the Lord, so walk in him. (Col. 2:6 ESV)

> But I say, walk by the Spirit, and you will not gratify the desires of the flesh. (Gal. 5:16 ESV)

> If we walk in the light, as he is in the light, we have fellowship with one another, and the blood of Jesus his Son cleanses us from all sin. (1 John 1:7 ESV)

It's in the Old Testament too. Adam and Eve took late-afternoon walks with God through the garden of Eden (see Gen. 3:8). And Genesis also says that "Enoch walked faithfully with God; then he was no more, because God took him away" (5:24 NIV). As I told the kids at the Bible study, that probably means he was taking a walk with the Lord one day when God said, "Hey, buddy, we're closer to My house than yours. Why don't you come home with Me today?" And he was caught up in the presence of the Lord.

Walking is about *consistency*. And that's also a big secret to the Christian life. It's beginning every day with Him and putting one foot in front of the other until you crawl between the sheets at night. Sometimes Christians are looking for some big emotional, transcendent experience. They tell themselves, "I'll go to this church service or that retreat and have an encounter with God, and everything will change."

And, yes, there really are such moments in our walk with the Lord, and we should treasure them. But the real "secret sauce" of Christianity is daily obedience to God. It's waking up, beginning the day with Him, and walking in step with Him all day long. In Psalm 25:5 David prayed, "Guide me in your truth and teach me, for you are God my Savior, and my hope is in you all day long" (NIV). In Psalm 5:3, he rolls out of bed and says, "Listen to my voice in the morning, LORD. Each morning I bring my requests to you and wait expectantly."

Eugene Peterson defined this daily habit as "a long obedience in the same direction."[1] It's walking by faith, not by feeling. Of course, since we are human, we're bound to experience some emotional highs and lows; we're at the lofty heights of the mountain one day, and then we crash and burn the next. But the Christian life at its best is when we walk (not run, not sprint) in fellowship with the indwelling Holy Spirit every day.

As nice as that might be, however, we're not in Heaven yet. There are dangers and warning signs on our walks. One of my friends had been looking forward to a hike by the Wenatchee River, near

Leavenworth, Washington, but he encountered yellow crime scene tape stretched across the trail. A sign said, "Trail closed. Bear activity ahead." He wanted to shrug it off and keep on going, but his wife said, "No, I don't think we need to walk in that direction today."

Wise woman! And that's the message of this first psalm. In our walk with God, we are presented with choices. We're not on auto-pilot, being steered from Heaven.

We have free will, and we have to make many decisions in the course of a day. We walk, but we must also choose to *not* walk on certain branching pathways.

The psalmist advises not to walk "in the counsel of the ungodly" (Ps. 1:1 NKJV).

Who are the ungodly? It doesn't necessarily mean an axe murderer or career criminal. In fact, the term might describe what we would call a garden-variety nonbeliever. They may actually be nice people who pay their bills, cut their grass, provide for their families, and clean up after their dogs. But on the weekends, church doesn't even cross their minds. They will say, "Oh, we're going to go to the mountains," or "We're spending the day at the beach." They're regular people, in a sense, but there's just no connection with God or His Word in their lives.

So in that sense, they're ungodly. You might say they are aimless. They live their days in a gray zone, taking what comes, not really sure what right and wrong are. They're just drifting through the months and years with no real direction, no biblical worldview, and walking on any random trail that opens before them.

The Bible is saying, "Don't walk in that sort of counsel. Don't follow their wandering steps. You can be friendly, compassionate, and helpful to a nonbelieving neighbor or friend, but be careful about tagging along behind them. Stick to the path God shows you in His Word, no matter what they say."

When you don't heed the warning signs, you might find yourself in the company of bears. Or worse.

Life isn't all rose petals and sunshine for a believer either. Even on the best paths, there will be bruises and wounds, rain and wind, heartbreaks and disappointments. I know. I've experienced them too. And so did David. But if you could somehow put a call through to him on some heavenly cell phone and ask for a word of advice, you might hear him advising, "Just make sure you keep walking with God, step by step, as best you can. It's not always an easy path (believe me!), but it leads to the best life on earth and the best place you could ever imagine in a trillion years."

A Page Torn from David's Journal

Blessed is the man
Who walks not in the counsel of the ungodly,
Nor stands in the path of sinners,
Nor sits in the seat of the scornful;
But his delight is in the law of the LORD,
And in His law he meditates day and night.
He shall be like a tree
Planted by the rivers of water,
That brings forth its fruit in its season,
Whose leaf also shall not wither;
And whatever he does shall prosper.

The ungodly are not so,
But are like the chaff which the wind drives away.
Therefore the ungodly shall not stand in the
        judgment,
Nor sinners in the congregation of the righteous.

For the LORD knows the way of the righteous,
But the way of the ungodly shall perish.

(Ps. 1 NKJV)

CHOOSING THE BEST PATH

Make me walk along the path of your commands,
for that is where my happiness is found.

Psalm 119:35

Inspired by Psalm 1

When God is absent from your life, you don't tread water and remain in the same place.

Some might tell themselves, *Well, I'm taking a break from church and the Christian life for a while. I want to go out and see what I've been missing. I can always come back and pick up where I left off.*

I was in Hawaii some years ago and ran into a guy who recognized me. We got into a conversation in which he told me he was "taking a vacation" from his Christian faith. That's another way of saying he was turning away from God. Fortunately, we were able to drill down on that, and we had prayer together as he turned back to the Lord.

But we can't "take a break" from church or a vacation from our faith.

Before you realize it, "where you were" may be miles away. Sadly, when you're not connected with God's Spirit, His Word, and His people, you go backward. You begin to regress.

I'm reminded of the verse in the book of Hebrews that warns us, "We must listen very carefully to the truth we have heard, or we may drift away from it" (2:1).

The word *drift* may sound easy and pleasant, but in this case it's not. Drifting may mean tragedy, heartache, or death.

Imagine you are in a rowboat rowing upstream on a very slow-moving river. After a while you get tired of rowing, so you lay down in the bottom of your boat and take a little nap. When you wake up, to your amazement, the scenery has completely changed. You don't even recognize it. You notice that the boat has begun moving faster, and you hear rapids approaching. Or a waterfall?

You think to yourself, *Where am I, and how did I get here?* The fact is, all you did was drift. It was easy. You didn't have to do anything at all. The current moved you.

That's what we see in Psalm 1. Watch the backward slide here:

> Blessed is the one
>> who does not walk in step with the wicked,
> or stand in the way that sinners take,
>> or sit in the company of mockers. (v. 1 NIV)

This is pretty much how temptation works. First you're walking, then you're standing, and then you're sitting.

Let's say you're on a diet, and you go out for a brisk walk every day. By chance, your route takes you by a Krispy Kreme Doughnuts outlet. As you approach, smelling the heavenly fragrance wafting into the cool morning air, you notice that the little sign is turned on, the red neon one that says, "Hot Doughnuts Now." Yes, you were on a walk, but now you are standing by a window with your face pressed against the glass looking in. Sure enough, the doughnuts are coming out of the oven. And then, before you have time to think about it, you are sitting at the counter, eating half a dozen doughnuts and washing them down with cold milk.

How did that happen? First you were walking, then you were standing, and you ended up sitting. That's how temptation works. You say, "I'm not going to do that." But then you stop and check it out. You play with the thought in your mind. And suddenly you're up to your ears in it.

Maybe, just maybe, it means you should change your walking route so you don't walk by Krispy Kreme when the doughnuts are hot.

When the psalmist speaks of the "seat of the scornful," he is talking about those who mock what is right. You see people on TV or social media who do that all the time, mocking and snickering at God's holy standards and the people who respect them. When you *become* that mocker, you know your rowboat has drifted far, far downstream—with the sound of a waterfall in your ears. You never want to be that person.

I used to mock Christians. I thought they were crazy. I made fun of them whenever I could because I didn't understand them. I didn't understand why anyone would want to carry a Bible in public. I didn't understand why people would want to talk about Jesus all the time. It seemed foreign and excessive and strange to me. But then came the day when I really heard the gospel clearly, and finally Christian behavior made sense to me.

And I became one of the people I had been mocking.

Happiness, then, begins with refusing to wander onto wrong paths and get caught up in doing wrong things.

Verse 2 gives us the contrast:

> But whose delight is in the law of the LORD,
> and who meditates on his law day and
> night. (NIV)

To put it another way, "He meditates on the Bible day and night." That's the secret. Don't live in the ungodly way, but meditate on the Word of God. *Delight* in it. The Hebrew word for "delight" has in it the idea of holding something extremely valuable in your hands. I love that. It's not something you *have* to do; it's something you *want* to do.

Charles Spurgeon, a great preacher from days gone by, made this statement: "Man must have some delight, some supreme pleasure. His heart was never meant to be a vacuum. If not filled with the best things, it will be filled with the unworthy and disappointing."[1]

What do you delight in? Seriously, what gives you joy? Some people delight in eating, while others even delight in exercise. (I don't understand the latter group of people, but I know they exist. They tell me about it—in great detail.) Others delight in criticizing. It's almost like a sport for them. The only exercise they get is jumping to conclusions and running down others.

But others delight in the Word of God. They begin and end their day with the Bible. What a wise and wonderful way to start and finish your day! Before you check your texts and emails, before you drop in to social media, before you catch the headlines about the horrendous happenings in our troubled nation and world, before all that ... you need to read the Bible and align your thoughts with your Creator's thoughts.

Try it. Try reading a verse or two of Scripture before you get into the shower.

The psalmist says that if you do that, you will be blessed. You will actually be a joyful person, no matter what your current circumstances are.

Sometimes when I'm going to sleep, I'll go over Scriptures I've memorized in years gone by—like the Lord's Prayer, Psalm 23, or Psalm 1.

When the psalmist says "meditate," don't picture Eastern meditation. This isn't sitting in a lotus position wearing Lululemon and trying to empty your mind. No, it's pretty much the opposite. In biblical meditation, you *fill your mind* with the Word of God. To meditate means to chew on a thought. You take time with a passage or a truth; you enjoy it, ponder it, contemplate it, and think of ways to put it to work in your life.

I find that when I take notes or write something in a journal, it stays in my mind longer. It sinks deeper into my memory. It isn't that hard. You jot a few things down in a little notebook or, these days, even speak them into your phone.

Are you in a difficult life situation? Have you found yourself in an unhappy job, in a troubled relationship, or with a challenging health condition? You can still be the blessed person described in Psalm 1.

In fact, your life can mirror the man or woman spoken about in verse 3:

> That person is like a tree planted by streams of
>   water,
> which yields its fruit in its season
> and whose leaf does not wither—
> whatever they do prospers. (NIV)

Fruit takes time to grow. If you pulled a chair up in front of a peach tree and said, "I'm going to watch the fruit grow today," you might get a little bored. You won't see any discernible growth whatsoever. But if you were to set up a camera and do time-lapse photography, you would see rapid growth and a beautiful transformation.

So as you abide in Christ and sink your roots deeply into Him, you will produce spiritual fruit in your life. You will have a freshness and a fragrance that others can't miss—and can't explain.

That's the happy life. That's the holy life. That's the road to Heaven. It's not the popular road, and it's not the easiest road, but it is the best road. The poet Robert Frost wrote about a road "less traveled," a place on his walk through the New England woods where the road divided and he had to choose. Finally, he picked the road less traveled. He concluded, "And that has made all the difference."[2]

It will make all the difference in your life too.

You will never regret choosing the best path. Not through the years of your life and not for eternity.

A Page Torn from David's Journal

Oh, the joys of those who do not follow evil men's advice, who do not hang around with sinners, scoffing at the things of God. But they delight in doing everything God wants them to, and day and night are always meditating on his laws and thinking about ways to follow him more closely.

They are like trees along a riverbank bearing luscious fruit each season without fail. Their leaves shall never wither, and all they do shall prosper.

But for sinners, what a different story! They blow away like chaff before the wind. They are not safe on Judgment Day; they shall not stand among the godly.

For the Lord watches over all the plans and paths of godly men, but the paths of the godless lead to doom.

(Ps. 1 TLB)

DON'T BE AFRAID

*The LORD is my light and my salvation—
whom shall I fear?
The LORD is the stronghold of my life—
of whom shall I be afraid?*

Psalm 27:1 (NIV)

Inspired by Psalm 27

When it comes to things people fear, where do we even begin?

The list stretches into the stratosphere.

Not long ago, I noticed some magazine's list of things that frighten Americans most. Right at the top was economic collapse. Many people remember the 2007–2008 global financial crisis—perhaps the most severe economic panic since the Great Depression. Some experts predict we are on the cusp of another one, and people are afraid of that.

With the world situation as it is, many people fear Russia using nuclear weapons against us, triggering a world war. It's a legitimate concern. As of 2024, Russia possesses 5,580 nuclear warheads—the largest such stockpile anywhere—and enough to incinerate the world many times over.[1] Then there's China, North Korea, Iran ...

But there are also personal fears, like the fear of someone you love with all your heart becoming seriously ill or even dying.

Your fears change as you age, of course. When you're young, it's the fear of the future. *Will I succeed in life? What career path should I pursue? Will I ever get married? How do we bring up kids in a world like we have now?*

And as you get even older, your fears change again: *How long will I live? Will my health hold out? Will I still be needed or even wanted?*

But then I read that the number-one fear of most people—even above death—is something called glossophobia. It's the fear of having to speak in public! Seriously, for many it would be a fate worse than death. So how does that work out? If the number-one fear is public speaking and the number two fear is death, that means most people would rather be lying in the casket than giving the eulogy at a funeral.

Fear can certainly impact your health. Studies have shown that heart attacks, ulcers, depression, nervous breakdowns, obesity, and even cancer can be related to anxiety, worry, and fear.

David faced times of intense fear in his life, and he wasn't ashamed to admit it and even write about it, as he did in Psalm 27.

He faced his fears, and we need to face ours.

We don't really know how Psalm 27 fits into the chronology of David's life, but I think we can safely assume it was written after he had taken care of business with Goliath, the nine-foot, six-inch Philistine freak who had challenged the Lord in the Valley of Elah.

I'm guessing he wrote this psalm after he'd been anointed as future king by Samuel and probably after the jealous King Saul had made him run for his life.

David was a courageous man. As I noted earlier, even as a teenager, he took on lions and bears that threatened his dad's sheep. I've never had to do that, but I did have some raccoons in my backyard not long ago. I wanted to throw something at them, but the only thing I had close at hand were those little mandarin oranges. (I think they're called Cuties.)

So I yelled at those raccoons in my most threatening voice and threw oranges at them.

The raccoons weren't impressed in the least, and every one of the oranges missed its target. I imagined one of the raccoons standing there with one paw on his hip, saying, "Really? Is that it? Is that the best you've got?"

David, however, didn't hesitate to take on the most threatening predators, reminding us that we need to face—and attack—the giants in our own lives.

Back on day 6, I talked about the giants of seemingly insurmountable problems. Here, I'm referring to giants that could be any number of things: A fear of failure. A scary report from the doctor. Or maybe a son or a daughter who's gone astray. Some people would rather face a charging bear than a family member who is breaking their heart. Whatever your giant—your obstacle—is, you need to face it rather than run from it or pretend it isn't there.

But you don't go after it alone.

Very early on in life, David's name soared to the top of Israel's Ten Most Wanted list. Though he had done nothing wrong, he became a fugitive with a price on his head. Even back then, Israel wasn't that big of a country, so it was a challenge finding a place to hide. Death stalked him everywhere. People who smiled at him one day would betray him the next.

But even as David was running for his life, he found some desolate corner of the kingdom and wrote these powerful words on a scroll:

> The LORD is my light and my salvation;
> Whom shall I fear?
> The LORD is the strength of my life;
> Of whom shall I be afraid? (Ps. 27:1 NKJV)

We need to overcome our fear. And the way we do it—the way David did it—is to replace fear with faith.

Fear and faith, you see, don't get along.

Do you have people in your orbit who don't mix well together? Maybe if you're going to go out to dinner, you'll say, "Let's invite Josh and Britney." And someone else will say, "That's okay, but then don't invite the Smiths, because they don't get along with Josh and Britney. They don't mix well. It's like oil and water."

That is a picture of faith and fear. They don't belong together. They don't mix. When faith walks in, fear walks out. When fear walks in, faith walks out. So you have to decide who you will invite to the party.

You can't seat them both at the same table.

You can't carry both of them as passengers in your car.

You can't keep both of them by your bedside at night.

You have to decide how you will respond when conflict or an unexpected challenge crosses your path—as it surely will. None of us can control what transpires on a given day. There's no weather map in the world that shows us all the fearful events on our horizon. We can't control such things, but we have everything to say about how we will react.

Have you noticed? The Christian life isn't a cakewalk; it's a conflict. It isn't a playground; it's a battleground. So we have to settle this issue deep in our souls. When the chips are down, are we going to live by fear or by faith?

It's always something, isn't it? Just when you get A and B settled a little bit, C walks in the back door. Fear is something that often hits us in the middle of the night—like three o'clock in the morning. Maybe it's a dream that wakes you up. But whatever it is, you start worrying and playing the what-if game in your mind. *What if this happens? What if I'm not able to do this? What if we run out of money? What happens if I get cancer?*

So what's the best thing to do in those situations?

When you're afraid in the dark, turn on the light. I'm not talking about the flashlight on your iPhone or the lamp on your nightstand. I'm talking about the Word of God—memorized, cherished, and tucked away in your heart.

David, possibly on a gloomy afternoon in the shadows of a spooky cavern on a dry hillside, asked, "The LORD is my light and my salvation; whom shall I fear?" (Ps. 27:1 NKJV).

My friend remembers being a little boy sleeping in a room with his big brother and arguing about having the bedroom door open a crack with the hall light on. His brother wanted it dark, but the little guy couldn't handle that. Somehow, that sliver of light represented safety, reassurance, and peace.

David said, "The Lord is that to me. He's the hall light shining into my dark bedroom. He's the sliver of warm light in the darkness of this cave. He's the shaft of sunlight cutting through the black clouds on a stormy day, reminding me that He is with me and that I'm not alone."

We have that same loving reassurance from the very same heavenly Father who comforted David. He's the One who tells us that everything will be okay. And how does He do that? Through His Holy Spirit, who reminds us of His unchanging Word.

Psalm 119:105 says, "Your word is a lamp to guide my feet and a light for my path." Another translation says: "Your words are a flashlight to light the path ahead of me and keep me from stumbling" (TLB).

Have you ever noticed how things look different when you turn on the light? So forget the whispers and threats you're hearing in the darkness, and remember what you heard from God's Word in the light of day.

Psalm 27 reminds us to face our fears in God's strength, not our own. David writes, "The LORD is the strength of my life" (v. 1 NKJV). Far too often we try to live the Christian life in our own strength—only to find ourselves flat on our backs and wondering what hit us.

The Hebrew word for "strength" speaks of a safe place, a fortified place, a stronghold. We don't deal with this much on the West Coast, but in other parts of our country, when the tornado sirens start wailing, people head for the basement or a less exposed room in the center of the house.

The Lord is our safe place. The Lord is our refuge and strong tower. When trouble comes, when danger threatens, when sorrow and grief descend like a tornado dropping out of the sky, we don't head for the basement—we run into His arms.

The apostle Paul reminds us, "I can do everything God asks me to with the help of Christ who gives me the strength and power" (Phil. 4:13 TLB). There might come a point (and truly, I hope there *will* come a point) when you will say, "This is bigger than me. I can't face this or overcome this problem—this failing marriage, these constant migraines, these mounting bills. I've tried and I have failed. So Lord, I come to You. I climb into Your fortress."

That's when you say with David, "Lord, You are the stronghold of my life."

I have been there. I have stood in that place, crying out to Him. And He was there in those frightening moments. I wouldn't have survived them without Him.

Here is the truth: When you get to the end of yourself, you get to the beginning of God.

Let God be the strength and stronghold of your life.

A Page Torn from David's Journal

Hear me as I pray, O LORD.
    Be merciful and answer me!
My heart has heard you say, "Come and talk with
        me."
    And my heart responds, "LORD, I am coming."
Do not turn your back on me.
    Do not reject your servant in anger.
    You have always been my helper....

Teach me how to live, O LORD.
   Lead me along the right path,
   for my enemies are waiting for me.
Do not let me fall into their hands.
   For they accuse me of things I've never done;
   with every breath they threaten me with violence.
Yet I am confident I will see the LORD's goodness
   while I am here in the land of the living.

Wait patiently for the LORD.
   Be brave and courageous.
   Yes, wait patiently for the LORD.

                                   (Ps. 27:7–9, 11–14)

ONE THING I SEEK MOST

I love the house where you live, O LORD,
the place where your glory dwells.

Psalm 26:8 (GNT)

Inspired by Psalm 27

In Psalm 57:7 David wrote: "My heart is fixed, O God, my heart is fixed" (KJV).

We might word it "settled" or "fastened" or "locked on like a laser beam."

What was his heart fixed on? David's whole life, from his earliest days, was focused on the Lord. He wasn't fickle. His objective—the overpowering desire of his heart—was clear. In fact, in Psalm 27:4 he said, "One thing I have desired of the LORD, that will I seek: that I may dwell in the house of the LORD all the days of my life, to behold the beauty of the LORD, and to inquire in His temple" (NKJV).

David knew where he was going in life, and one thing was more important to him than anything else: to be as close to God as he could possibly be, in the dwelling place of the Lord.

Again, he said, "One thing I have desired of the Lord."

One thing.

No doubt he also wanted things that all of us want: love, marriage, a family, friends, meaningful work, and maybe a little comfort here and there. But above and beyond and through all those other natural human desires, David wanted the Lord. He wanted to be as close as he could get to his Creator.

In Psalm 26:8, he tells God, "I love the house where you live, O LORD, the place where your glory dwells" (GNT).

In Psalm 61:4, he cries out, "Let me dwell in your tent forever! Let me take refuge under the shelter of your wings!" (ESV).

David longed to "dwell in the house of the LORD" and to "behold [His] beauty ... in His temple" (Ps. 27:4 NKJV). Back in Old Testament days, the temple—and, before that, the tabernacle or the tent—was the place where people would meet God. David was essentially saying, "I wish I could edge up as close as I could get to the presence of the Lord, and just stay there day and night." In that tabernacle or temple was the inner sanctum, the holy of holies, where only the high priest could enter.

David was saying, "I wish there was a way I could just live there, as close to His presence as I could possibly get, for the rest of my days."

That was David's "one thing."

The apostle Paul had "one thing" in his life too. In the book of Philippians, he wrote, "I am bringing all my energies to bear on this *one thing*: Forgetting the past and looking forward to what lies ahead, I strain to reach the end of the race and receive the prize for which God is calling us up to heaven because of what Christ Jesus did for us" (3:13–14 TLB).

In Luke 10:41–42, the Lord Jesus had to gently correct His friend Martha when she complained about how her sister, Mary, had camped at His feet, soaking up every word, instead of chopping olives in the kitchen. He said, "Martha, dear friend, you are so upset over all these details! There is really only *one thing* worth being concerned about. Mary has discovered it—and I won't take it away from her!" (TLB).

We can all identify with Martha. Most of our lives are loaded down with details—many of them important to us. But Jesus says, "There is really only one thing worth being concerned about. And it is your relationship with Me."

We all have to tend to a lot of important things. So did Paul. So did David. So did Martha. But if we know the Lord, there needs to be one central focus in our hearts—our relationship with Him.

We don't have a tabernacle or temple today, but many of us love being at church. We love the worship. We love the Bible study and prayer. We love seeing God work. And after the service, we like to hang out and just spend time with each other. We develop friendships and relationships. We're all intertwined.

That's what it's all about! It's a community. The Holy Spirit gives us that strong desire to be with God's people, and sometimes we just can't get enough of it. We've come to know the value of fellowship.

Yet today, as Christians, we can enter into "the holy of holies" twenty-four hours a day, 365 days a year. Hebrews 10:19–22 says:

> Dear brothers and sisters, we can boldly enter heaven's Most Holy Place because of the blood of Jesus. By his death, Jesus opened a new and life-giving way

> through the curtain into the Most Holy Place. And
> since we have a great High Priest who rules over
> God's house, let us go right into the presence of
> God with sincere hearts fully trusting him.

That is such good news! You don't have to be in the building—"the temple" or even a church—to enjoy the presence of the Lord.

If you're stuck commuting every day on the freeway, driving for an hour and a half or two hours, you can make your car a sanctuary! Put on some praise music. Listen to Scripture on a Bible program. Your car can be a temple of worship to the Lord.

Just start talking to Him. Draw near to Him. Open your heart and thoughts to Him. He's always on the line. Spend some time in His presence, soak it up, and worship Him. There may be many things going on in your day, but make this the *one thing*—the most important purpose in your life.

No, you probably shouldn't lift up your hands while you're worshipping on the freeway. It's best to keep your hands on the wheel. Even so, you can keep company with the mighty God of the universe who loves you, and it will make all the difference in your day.

Deep down, that's what David wanted. *One thing in life.* And yes, tragically, there were seasons in his life when he lost that focus.

But he always, always came back.

And that's what made him "a man after [God's] own heart."

A Page Torn from David's Journal

O God, listen to my cry!
   Hear my prayer!
From the ends of the earth,
   I cry to you for help
   when my heart is overwhelmed.
Lead me to the towering rock of safety,
   for you are my safe refuge,
   a fortress where my enemies cannot reach me
Let me live forever in your sanctuary,
   safe beneath the shelter of your wings!

For you have heard my vows, O God.
   You have given me an inheritance reserved for
      those who fear your name.

(Ps. 61:1–5)

THE MAIN THING

*The one thing I want from God, the thing I seek most
of all, is the privilege of meditating in his Temple,
living in his presence every day of my life.*

Psalm 27:4 (TLB)

Inspired by Psalm 27

It was Stephen Covey who wrote, "The main thing is to keep the main thing the main thing."[1]

David hadn't read any of Covey's books, but it's a principle he practiced anyway. Coming back to Psalm 27:4 we read:

> One thing I have asked of the LORD,
>   that will I seek after:
> that I may dwell in the house of the LORD
>   all the days of my life,
> to gaze upon the beauty of the LORD,
>   and to inquire in His temple. (ESV)

One of the dangers everyone faces in life is to permit the "urgent" things to crowd out the most important things. You know how that works: You have a seemingly endless list of errands to run all over town, and then, at the end of the day, you realize you haven't once opened God's Word or opened your heart to the Lord in prayer. Or maybe (like Martha) you're busy in the kitchen trying to get a gourmet meal prepared before the company arrives. But out of the corner of your eye, you notice that your ten-year-old is really troubled about something and needs to talk. Deep down, you know the dinner can wait and the company can wait and that sitting down with your child may be the most important thing you do all day.

It's the same with seeking the Lord.

Some people are busy with activities or family plans and will say, "I don't really feel like I need to go to church. I can commune with God when I'm in the outdoors. Besides, the church has so many problems."

Yes, it does.

It's a package deal: If you have people, you have problems. If you didn't have people, the church would have no problems at all. But it wouldn't be the church! Because the church is filled with people like you and me, we run into difficulties and disappointments and disagreements. But that problem is as old as the idea of church itself. The churches described in 1 and 2 Corinthians, 1 and 2 Timothy, Galatians, the epistles of John, and Revelation had all kinds of issues—some that would curl your hair!

We mess everything up, but Jesus Himself established the church. And He gives a beautiful promise when He tells us that when two or three gather in His name, He is there among us.

God manifests His presence in a special way when we gather for worship or Bible study. In these days, many people watch church services online, in their homes, in their pajamas. And we're all grateful for those opportunities on occasion. But there is something very special—some added blessing and joy—when you worship God in company with others.

If you aren't part of a church family, I encourage you to find a good Bible-teaching, Jesus-loving fellowship and join them in worship. You need the church, and the church needs you. We are meant for community, and we should not try to live our Christian life in isolation, apart from other believers.

Have you ever noticed how when the disciples asked Jesus, "Lord, would you teach us to pray?" He gave them what we call the Lord's Prayer? But how does it begin?

"*Our* Father in heaven" (Matt. 6:9 NKJV).

Not "*My* Father in heaven."

Later in the prayer, Jesus says to pray, "Give *us* this day our daily bread" (v. 11 NKJV).

Jesus is showing us the importance and power of praying together.

It's not just "one more thing" in life. It is the main thing.

We need God and we need each other.

If we don't focus on that one thing, we'll end up doing everything and accomplishing nothing.

Later in Psalm 27, David writes:

> Hear, O LORD, when I cry aloud;
>   be gracious to me and answer me!
> You have said, "Seek My face,"
> My heart says to you,
>   "Your face, LORD, do I seek."
> Hide not your face from me.

> Turn not your servant away in anger,
>   O you who have been my help.
> Cast me not off; forsake me not,
>   O God of my salvation!
> For my father and my mother have forsaken me,
>   but the LORD will take me in. (vv. 7–10 ESV)

You have a Father in Heaven who loves you and always has time for you.

In the New Living Translation, verse 8 reads: "My heart has heard you say, 'Come and talk with me.' And my heart responds, 'LORD, I am coming.'"

How beautiful is that? Wherever David was, whether he was walking under the stars or hiding in the rocks and brambles from Saul, he heard the voice of God. And it moved David's heart. He found himself replying, "Yes! Yes, Lord, let's talk. I need You, and I have missed You."

Did your earthly dad ever say to you, "Let's talk, son," or "Come walk with me for a while, daughter, and tell me about your day"? Those would be sweet words to hear. But many of us have never heard them. Some of us may have had fathers who merely tolerated us or basically ignored us.

We know from 1 Samuel 16 that David wasn't really appreciated by his dad. It's obvious that Jesse favored his older sons over David, "the runt" (1 Sam. 16:11 MSG).

Was that why he made this statement in Psalm 27:10: "My father and my mother have forsaken me, but the LORD will take me in" (ESV)?

I personally relate to this verse. My mom was married and divorced seven times, so I wasn't with her for a good part of my childhood. She would send me to live with my grandparents and aunts and uncles, and I did a couple of stints in military school, where I lived on campus. So I really missed my mom, and I didn't know who my father was.

I was married to Cathe at twenty-one, and we had our first son, Christopher. At twenty-two I went looking for my dad. One day I said to Cathe, "Christopher should meet his biological grandfather." So I went to my mom and asked if he was still alive.

She said he was. I asked if she knew where he was, and she said she did. So I told her, "I'm going to introduce Christopher to him."

He ran a dry-cleaning shop, and he was standing at the counter when I walked through the door with my baby.

"Hi," I said. "I'm Greg."

He said, "I know who you are." And he never stepped out from behind the counter.

I held up Christopher and said, "This is your grandson."

He said, "Oh. Okay." He never made a move to hold Christopher or show any interest in him at all.

So I finally said, "Well, okay. Goodbye." And we left.

Later I said to Cathe, "That's not my biological father! I don't know who it is, but it ain't him!" My mother had lied to me. He wasn't my dad. In fact, she had never had a relationship with my real dad. It was just a one-night stand.

I don't know what your relationship with your mom and dad was or is like. If you had loving, hands-on parents, you should thank God for them every day. But if, like millions of men and women across our country, you never knew your dad or mom or never had a relationship with them, then remember this: If your father and mother abandoned you or were indifferent to you, you have a Father in Heaven who has promised to never abandon you, who has never been indifferent toward you for one millisecond, and who loves you beyond what any human language can express.

In Hebrews 13:5, He declares, "I will never fail you. I will never abandon you."

That's absolutely clear enough in ten words. But if you would like the expanded version, it goes like this:

> I WILL NEVER [under any circumstances] DESERT YOU [nor give you up nor leave you without support, nor will I in any degree leave you helpless], NOR WILL I FORSAKE or LET YOU DOWN or RELAX MY HOLD ON YOU [assuredly not]!" (AMP)

God never did leave David; it was David who left God.

But that wasn't the end of the story. David repented and came back. And His heavenly Father was there waiting for him.

A PAGE TORN FROM DAVID'S JOURNAL

> Listen to my pleading, Lord! Be merciful and send the help I need.

> My heart has heard you say, "Come and talk with me, O my people." And my heart responds, "Lord, I am coming."

Oh, do not hide yourself when I am trying to find you. Do not angrily reject your servant. You have been my help in all my trials before; don't leave me now. Don't forsake me, O God of my salvation. For if my father and mother should abandon me, you would welcome and comfort me.

Tell me what to do, O Lord, and make it plain because I am surrounded by waiting enemies. Don't let them get me, Lord! Don't let me fall into their hands! For they accuse me of things I never did, and all the while are plotting cruelty. I am expecting the Lord to rescue me again, so that once again I will see his goodness to me here in the land of the living.

(Ps. 27:7–13 TLB)

—— DAY 15 ——

GOD USES NEEDY PEOPLE

As for me, since I am poor and needy,
let the Lord keep me in his thoughts.

Psalm 40:17

Inspired by Psalm 40

In many ways, David was the polar opposite of King Saul.

Saul came from a family where he was probably loved and valued, and David from a family where he was evidently neglected, belittled, even disliked. Saul had Hollywood handsomeness—star material. David was a relatively ordinary shepherd boy, though good-looking. Saul was attractive on the outside, but inside he was vain, shallow, and devoid of true integrity. In contrast, David, though he was young, had a deep spiritual life and an intense devotion to God.

And he never seemed overly impressed with himself.

Recall what Paul wrote to the believers in Corinth:

> Remember, dear brothers and sisters, that few of
> you were wise in the world's eyes or powerful or

> wealthy when God called you. Instead, God chose
> things the world considers foolish in order to shame
> those who think they are wise. And he chose things
> that are powerless to shame those who are power-
> ful. God chose things despised by the world, things
> counted as nothing at all, and used them to bring
> to nothing what the world considers important.
> (1 Cor. 1:26–28)

It's true, isn't it? But that's hard for us to admit. We don't like to think of ourselves as weak. We like to think of ourselves as strong and bright and capable.

Years ago, I had the opportunity to be interviewed by the late, great radio personality Larry King. The discussion turned to suffering, and Larry asked why it even existed in our world in the first place.

I told him that God can use suffering in our lives, often to bring us to faith. I mentioned a C. S. Lewis quote about how God "whispers to us in our pleasures ... but shouts in our pain."[1]

I then related a story about a lady who had breast cancer and had come to our church office the previous Sunday morning after the first service. She told me how this tragedy had gotten her attention, and so she was turning to God.

Larry interrupted me and said, "How do you know it's not a crutch? ... You know, there's a believer in every foxhole."

I responded, "Thank God for that crutch! Larry, He's not a crutch to me—He's a whole hospital!"[2]

I am not ashamed to admit that I'm weak and need God. And the person who is afraid to admit that is really a fool.

But we forget that sometimes. We get caught up in the idea that fame and fashion and style and charisma—or people liking our posts on social media—are the most important things in life. We always wish some big-time, important people would get saved. "Man, I wish a movie star would come to Christ. Or a rock star. Or some prominent politician or news anchor—or someone really well-known or impressive. Then we could say, 'So-and-so is on *our* side now.'"

The truth is, God will save anyone who calls upon Him in faith. But in many cases, those who do call are just regular, everyday sorts of people who have a hunger for God and realize their need for a Savior. These are men and women and boys and girls who may not be the most talented or brilliant people to walk the planet. They may not be bodybuilders or cover girls. They may not be the type to survive six months on *Jeopardy*. They're just people who come to God in their weakness and say, "Lord, I need You! And if You can use me, here I am. I'm available."

Refusing to rely on human resources, they freely admit their weakness and faults, but they allow God to work with and through them in a spectacular, supernatural way.

That's good news for us ordinary people.

That's good news for anyone who wants God to use them.

The Lord sometimes picks men and women that you and I would never pick for prominent kingdom roles! He draws people from the back of the line. He plucks people out of obscurity.

Billy Graham was a dairy farmer, known to the local populace simply as Billy Frank. And God raised him up to be the greatest evangelist the world has ever seen.

God delights to use commonplace people and do extraordinary works through their lives. It makes sense, doesn't it? When a nonspectacular person ends up doing amazingly spectacular things ... guess who gets the glory?

David was a truly spiritual man. Not some plastic, surfacy, scripted persona. He was the real deal. Genuine through and through. When we see pictures of him in the Bible, there are no filters or special effects to make him look more appealing. We see David at his highest highs and lowest lows. That's what I like about him.

When David was upset, he told the Lord all about it. You can see it again and again in the psalms. He talked plainly about how he felt about things and didn't try to hide it or smooth it over with religious-sounding words. But then a few lines down in the same psalm he would come right back and remind himself of the love and faithfulness of his God. When you read psalms like that, you can relate to this guy. This was a real human being who put on his sandals one foot at a time.

And God was pleased to use him in a mighty way.

I can remember times of being at the late Billy and Ruth Graham's house, hanging around with them and watching them enjoy life, laugh, tease each other, and have fun. Just regular, relaxed people like you'd meet in your own church.

The most spiritual people I have ever met—and I've had the opportunity to meet some wonderful, godly people all over the world—have always been down-to-earth, normal, real people. You can spot phony, tacked-on spirituality a mile away, and the truth is, it's not spirituality at all. It's just an act. And God isn't impressed with that one bit.

David was authentic. If you want to really see who this man was and what made him tick, just read Psalms. It's all there for you, a realistic portrait of his life.

He struggled with sin just like you and me. And he wrote about it for all the world to see!

> My problems go from bad to worse. Oh, save me
> from them all! See my sorrows; feel my pain; for-
> give my sins. (Ps. 25:17–18 TLB)

> For troubles without number surround me;
>   my sins have overtaken me, and I cannot see.
> They are more than the hairs of my head,
>   and my heart fails within me. (Ps. 40:12 NIV)

> Don't keep looking at my sins.
>   Remove the stain of my guilt. (Ps. 51:9)

Does that sound like somebody who wanted a perfect profile on Facebook? For most of his life, David kept his heart wide open to the Lord. He stayed real. Yes, he committed some terrible sins, but he kept coming back to the Lord, seeking His face all over again.

In God's kingdom, weakness and failure don't disqualify us.

What disqualifies us is pride—and an indifferent heart toward God.

A Page Torn from David's Journal

I waited patiently for the LORD to help me,
  and he turned to me and heard my cry.
He lifted me out of the pit of despair,
  out of the mud and the mire.
He set my feet on solid ground
  and steadied me as I walked along.
He has given me a new song to sing,
  a hymn of praise to our God.
Many will see what he has done and be amazed.
  They will put their trust in the LORD.

(Ps. 40:1–3)

A Warning to Stay Alert

*David had obeyed God during his entire life except
for the affair concerning Uriah the Hittite.*

1 Kings 15:5 (TLB)

Inspired by 2 Samuel 11; Psalm 32

All his life, since he was a lonely teenager strumming his little harp and looking after his dad's sheep, David had lived by godly priorities. He loved the Lord, and the Lord loved him. Even though he walked through many dark valleys and experienced heartbreaks and disappointments beyond counting, for most of his years he lived a consistent, godly life.

The writer of 1 Kings noted: "For David had lived an exemplary life before GOD all his days, not going off on his own in willful defiance of GOD's clear directions" (1 Kings 15:5 MSG).

When he had opportunity to take matters into his own hands and take revenge against his bitter enemy Saul, he refused to strike down the one he referred to as "the Lord's anointed." No, David wasn't perfect (none of us are), but he had his priorities in order. His life was indeed "a long obedience in the same direction."[1]

Even when he had to spend long days hiding from his enemy in a gloomy cave, David wrote:

> My heart, O God, is steadfast,
>> my heart is steadfast;
>> I will sing and make music.
> Awake, my soul!
>> Awake, harp and lyre!
>> I will awaken the dawn. (Ps. 57:7–8 NIV)

Essentially, he was saying, "I'm going to stick with my morning devotions even in the back of this awful cave. I'm going to be up with the sun praising the Lord, no matter my circumstances."

When David finally became king after long years of waiting, he brought those same standards and values into governing Israel. The people were prospering as never before, and they loved him. He was on a roll.

But twenty years into his reign, when David was fifty, something went sideways.

It started with a lustful look, and it became a national scandal. Even people who don't know much about the Bible can say David's name and associate him with two other names: Goliath and Bathsheba. The first was David's greatest victory, and the second his most devastating defeat. As much as the name of David has been revered through the years, most everyone knows about David's great sin—the lowest valley in his life to that point.

These stories are in the Bible for a reason. We see the sin and the following consequences in great detail, and it's like a warning light blinking in the night: Take care! Be careful!

The account of David and Bathsheba shows us that even though you have been walking closely with the Lord for a long, long time, you still are vulnerable to falling.

What an important truth!

The Bible says, "If you think you are standing firm, be careful that you don't fall!" (1 Cor. 10:12 NIV). Another version puts it this way: "Don't be so naive and self-confident. You're not exempt. You could fall flat on your face as easily as anyone else. Forget about self-confidence; it's useless. Cultivate God-confidence" (MSG).

The next time you hear about someone prominent falling into sexual sin, the last thing you should allow yourself to think or say is, "I would never do that. That would never happen with me."

Don't be so sure.

Saying "never" puts you on very shaky footing.

You remember that it was Peter in the upper room who said in the presence of Christ and the other disciples, "They'll all deny You, but I will never deny You." Don't ever say anything like that. When we are under the control of our old nature, without the guidance and protection of the Holy Spirit, we are capable of any number of shameful things. Rather, our attitude should be, "Oh, God, help me. Don't let me take one step down that road! Lord, let me stay close to You today."

You know the story. David had sent General Joab and the troops into battle but decided to stay home and take it easy. Second Samuel 11:1 captures the scene like this:

> In the spring of the year, when kings normally
> go out to war, David sent Joab and the Israelite
> army to fight the Ammonites. They destroyed the
> Ammonite army and laid siege to the city of Rabbah.
> However, David stayed behind in Jerusalem.

That's a big "however."

By all rights, David should have been leading the troops. Just having him out front would have energized and inspired his men ten times over. "He's here! Praise God, the giant-killer is leading us! Follow the king!"

Nevertheless, for whatever reason, the king stayed home, and he soon found himself idle and restless. David was resting when he should have been fighting. He was kicking back, taking a little time off. And by the way, there's nothing wrong with taking some time off. But as we've already seen, you can't take a spiritual vacation. The spiritual battle rages all day and all night long. It's even raging when you're asleep, right? There are no holidays from fighting temptation and resisting the Evil One.

Second Samuel 11 goes on to describe a sad and sordid scene. While walking on his palace rooftop, David was enflamed by lust for a woman he had seen bathing in one of the homes below. He sent for her, brought her into the king's bedroom, and slept with her. He did this even though he knew she was the wife of one of his loyal soldiers who was out on the battlefield at that very moment, fighting the Lord's battles.

David was being idle and slothful, and his armor was off—in more ways than one. At the time when kings led their soldiers into battle, David was taking long naps. In a sense, he had already set himself up for an attack.

Our greatest battles don't necessarily come when we're working hard. They often come when we have some leisure time or when we're bored. I once heard Alan Redpath, the great British preacher, make this statement: "Times of leisure are to be more dreaded than those of the most strenuous toil."

David had lowered his guard, underestimating Satan, his real enemy.

The apostle Peter, who could look back on his own devastating fall, wrote:

> Stay alert! Watch out for your great enemy, the
> devil. He prowls around like a roaring lion, looking
> for someone to devour. Stand firm against him, and
> be strong in your faith. Remember that your family
> of believers all over the world is going through the
> same kind of suffering you are. (1 Pet. 5:8–9)

Don't you love that? Stay awake! Stay alert! Stand firm! And remember that when it comes to temptation and the lure of sin in your life, you aren't the Lone Ranger. Christians *all over the world* are fighting that same battle right now—at this very moment—and trusting in the same Savior and Protector we do. I find that incredibly comforting. Followers of Jesus from Ontario to Peru, from Finland to Nepal, are standing against the Enemy and resisting his attacks. It makes me want to stand with them!

One of Satan's approaches is to make us think we can compromise a little without actually falling into sin. We tell ourselves, "I can handle this. I can cut this little corner and make this little compromise. I'm pretty strong. I've had a good run. It'll be okay."

But maybe it won't be okay.

I read about an eighty-year-old man in Virginia who was bitten by a rattlesnake and died. Upon first hearing this story, you might say, "What's shocking about that? Rattlesnake bites do kill people, and he was eighty years old."

As it turns out, however, this particular man was a highly respected authority on snakes, particularly rattlesnakes. He had been around them and studied them since childhood. His specialty was studying the habits of timber rattlers in their mountain habitat.

He would go out into the wild and find these snakes where no one else could find them. He was literally an expert on all things concerning rattlesnakes. And then he ended up getting bit by one.

How did that happen? It seems he was keeping one in captivity as a pet. Apparently, he let down his guard for a minute, and it bit him. He had been bitten before and survived, so he may have thought, *I can handle this. It will be okay.*

But it wasn't okay. He died before he could get medical attention, leaving a grieving widow behind.

I think it's the same way with sin. We tell ourselves, *I can handle this. I'll never capitulate to this sin. I'll never fall in this area.* David might even have been thinking this on the roof of his palace when he inadvertently saw the beautiful woman bathing. But instead of looking away, he may have rationalized, *Well, God is the author of beauty, so I'll just enjoy this for a moment or two. No harm done.*

He thought it would be okay. He thought he could handle it. But then the snake bit him, and life was never the same after that moment.

Ironically, David's fall came after great spiritual success. That seems to be our Enemy's modus operandi.

When did Jesus get attacked by the Devil? Right after He had been baptized by his cousin, John the Baptist, in the Jordan River. What an amazing scene. The heavens opened, and the Spirit of God came down in the form of a beautiful dove, lighting on His shoulder. And the voice from Heaven said, "This is My beloved Son, in whom I am well pleased" (Matt. 3:17 NKJV).

You can almost hear the angels singing in the background. It was such an exalted moment. But then we read, "Immediately the Holy Spirit urged Jesus into the desert. There, for forty days, alone except for desert animals, he was subjected to Satan's temptations to sin" (Mark 1:12–13 TLB).

After the dove came the Devil. After the blessing came the attack. The two often go hand in hand. The Devil waits for the moment when he thinks we're the most vulnerable, when we might lower our guard spiritually.

David had it right in Psalm 57, when he sang that a steadfast heart and a song of praise are the best way to start a day (v.7). On the day he fell, he might have missed that opportunity and privilege.

But you and I don't have to.

A PAGE TORN FROM DAVID'S JOURNAL

Finally, I confessed all my sins to you
    and stopped trying to hide my guilt.

I said to myself, "I will confess my rebellion to the
     LORD."
    And you forgave me! All my guilt is gone.

Therefore, let all the godly pray to you while there is
     still time,
    that they may not drown in the floodwaters of
     judgment.
For you are my hiding place;
    you protect me from trouble.
    You surround me with songs of victory.

The LORD says, "I will guide you along the best
     pathway for your life.
    I will advise you and watch over you.
Do not be like a senseless horse or mule
    that needs a bit and bridle to keep it under
     control."

Many sorrows come to the wicked,
    but unfailing love surrounds those who trust the
     LORD.
So rejoice in the LORD and be glad, all you who
     obey him!
    Shout for joy, all you whose hearts are pure!

(Ps. 32:5–11)

MISERY AND RELEASE

For I admit my shameful deed—it haunts me day and night. It is
against you and you alone I sinned and did this terrible thing.

Psalm 51:3–4 (TLB)

Inspired by 2 Samuel 11; Psalms 32 and 51

In 2 Samuel 11:27, we read something we never want to learn about ourselves.

The Bible says, "The thing that David had done displeased the LORD" (ESV).

What had he done? He had committed adultery with another man's wife—the wife of his own brave and loyal soldier—tried to cover up the sin, and then, when that wouldn't wash, arranged to have that soldier killed in battle.

It was a cruel, cold-blooded thing to do, and David may have told himself that no one knew. But General Joab knew. Undoubtedly, Bathsheba knew. The Lord knew. And of course David knew. And the memory of what he had done was eating him alive.

This was far, far worse than running from Saul and hiding in the wilderness. At least then he had the sense of his Lord's presence and blessing. But now? He probably tried to put the Lord out of his mind altogether.

Difficult as it may be to conceive, David was a real believer during all this adultery, intrigue, and murder. A believer, but a disobedient believer. As a result, he found himself in a living death—an intolerable place where he had not yet repented of his sin and his sin had not yet gone public.

Later, after he confessed to the Lord and the deed was known, he wrote two psalms—Psalms 32 and 51. Psalm 32 describes the futility and utter misery of sin that is hidden and unconfessed.

Remember, David was a man who had walked and talked with God since childhood. He could have easily written the lines his friend Asaph penned in Psalm 73:28:

> As for me, how good it is to be near God!
>   I have made the Sovereign LORD my shelter,
>   and I will tell everyone about the wonderful
>   things you do.

But after the Bathsheba incident, David lived with hidden sin and fought the conviction of the Holy Spirit for twelve horrible months.

After the fact and looking back, he wrote about that experience in Psalm 32:3–4. And by the way, that took courage too. He could have minimized that whole dark season of his life or swept it under the rug. But thankfully for us, he committed the experience to a scroll, allowing people like us—on the other side of the world and three thousand years later—to learn from his pain and humiliation.

When I refused to confess my sin,
　my body wasted away,
　and I groaned all day long.
Day and night your hand of discipline was heavy
　　　on me.
　My strength evaporated like water in the summer
　　　heat.

The Message paraphrases it like this:

When I kept it all inside,
　my bones turned to powder,
　my words became daylong groans.

The pressure never let up;
　all the juices of my life dried up.

Wow. What a perfect description of what it's like to live an unconfessed sin. *The pressure never lets up.* Most of us—probably all of us—have experienced this feeling in some way, shape, or form: when you know you have sinned against the Lord, when you know you have grieved His Holy Spirit and yet haven't confessed your sin, it just eats at you.

In a strange way, however, that's good news. It's eating at you because it doesn't belong in the life of a child of God. It is something dark and alien, and everything in you hates having that broken fellowship with the Lord.

In Isaiah, the prophet writes: "It's your sins that have cut you off from God. Because of your sins, he has turned away and will not listen anymore" (59:2).

And if you have known the Lord, walked with the Lord, sung to the Lord, and crowded up close to the Lord in your lifetime, being cut off from Him is an unbearable place to be.

Finally, after being fearlessly confronted by Nathan, God's prophet, the dam broke. David said, "I have sinned against the LORD" (2 Sam. 12:13 NIV). Not just against Bathsheba. Not just against Uriah. Not just against the people he ruled who had admired him and counted on him. But *the Lord*—his loving Savior, shepherd and friend. In Psalm 32:5 he wrote:

> Finally, I confessed all my sins to you
>   and stopped trying to hide my guilt.
> I said to myself, "I will confess my rebellion to the
>   LORD."
>   And you forgave me! All my guilt is gone.

Yes, the guilt was gone. And that was wonderful. But the consequences of David's sin remained. Like a rock dropped into the middle of a still pool, the ripples rolled out far and wide for years and generations.

The Bible makes it clear that God disciplines those He loves. This discipline and conviction in David's life was a sign he was a child of God. The book of Hebrews puts it down in black and white.

> "My child, don't make light of the LORD's
>   discipline,
>   and don't give up when he corrects you.
> For the LORD disciplines those he loves,
>   and he punishes each one he accepts as his
>   child."

As you endure this divine discipline, remember that God is treating you as his own children. Whoever heard of a child who is never disciplined by its father? If God doesn't discipline you as he does all of his children, it means that you are illegitimate and are not really his children at all. (12:5–8)

David was certainly God's child. And he had to face up to the consequences of his actions. Ironically, he actually wrote about it back in Psalm 23:4: "Even when I walk through the darkest valley, I will not be afraid, for you are close beside me. Your rod and your staff protect and comfort me."

A shepherd in those days had two primary instruments in the tending of sheep: the rod and the staff. The staff was used for pulling wayward lambs out of the rocks and bushes and swampy places. The rod was used to fight off predators and occasionally used on a straying sheep. A shepherd generally would not use a rod on his sheep; he'd rather use his staff to guide them and pull them out of trouble. But if one of those little lambs wavered, perhaps leading other lambs astray, the shepherd would use the rod.

God's *discipline* is reserved for God's own kids—the sons and daughters He loves.

Have you ever seen someone's child misbehaving, maybe in the grocery store or mall? It's hard to watch. Some kids have no manners at all and show no respect for their parents or anyone else. There are times when I wish I could discipline someone else's child, but I can't do that, and I wouldn't do that. It's not my right, and I could get in trouble for it. But God will discipline His own children.

Why? Hebrews 12 has the answer again. The writer says in verse 10 that, yes, it is painful at the time, "but afterward there will be a peaceful harvest of right living for those who are trained in this way" (v. 11). Another version says, "Afterwards we can see the result, a quiet growth in grace and character" (TLB).

What do we learn from this difficult true story in Scripture? Number one, we should daily seek the Lord's protection so we will not wander off onto dangerous paths or fall into life-devastating sins. But, second, if we do sin, if we do fall, there is only one correct response to being caught in sin.

And to David's credit, he said the right thing: "I have sinned."

What he did was wrong and horrible, and he would face the repercussions of his actions for years to come. But finally, he did admit his sin. He did come clean.

If the prophet Nathan had confronted another king of that era the way he confronted David, the prophet might have been executed on the spot. But David bowed his head and said, "You are right."

When King Saul was confronted with his sin, he just dug in deeper and sinned more. When David was confronted with his sin, he came clean, admitted it, and repented before God.

And because he did, David was given a second chance in his life. As devastating as his story sounds, David did make a comeback. There was a lot of turmoil and sadness to come, but ultimately, his life ended well.

And what about Bathsheba? Did she bear some culpability for what happened between her and David? The Bible really doesn't say. But here's the shocker: Bathsheba, the wife of Uriah and David, made it into the messianic line of Jesus Christ!

Matthew 1:6 states that "David was the father of Solomon, whose mother had been Uriah's wife" (NIV).

When you look at the family line of David, you find not only Bathsheba but also two other women, Tamar and Rahab, who were both prostitutes who turned to God. So what does this mean? It means God gives second chances. And third chances. And hundredth chances. It means God can bring good out of even the most heart-breaking circumstances.

Think of it! Eventually, out of the union of David and Bathsheba, Solomon was born—one of the wisest men who ever lived and the author of three books of our Bible. But beyond that, the Lord Jesus Christ Himself was born from the same family line. And how good that the name of Uriah, that loyal soldier of Israel, also made it into the New Testament. Bathsheba was listed as his wife.

Maybe as you read these words you are in need of a second chance. It might be that you have been unfaithful in your marriage. Maybe you have broken up a home. Maybe you've been living a sexually impure life. Or perhaps it is something else from your past that causes you grief every time you think of it.

Run to Him. Tell Him everything. And accept His complete and total forgiveness.

Our amazing Lord knows how to work the broken ends of our life stories into good, for His glory.

A Page Torn from David's Journal

> Bless the LORD, O my soul;
> And all that is within me, bless His holy name!
> Bless the LORD, O my soul,
> And forget not all His benefits:
> Who forgives all your iniquities,
> Who heals all your diseases,
> Who redeems your life from destruction,
> Who crowns you with lovingkindness and tender
>   mercies....
>
> The LORD is merciful and gracious,
> Slow to anger, and abounding in mercy.
> He will not always strive with us,
> Nor will He keep His anger forever.
> He has not dealt with us according to our sins,
> Nor punished us according to our iniquities.
>
> For as the heavens are high above the earth,
> So great is His mercy toward those who fear Him;
> As far as the east is from the west,
> So far has He removed our transgressions from us.

(Ps. 103:1–4, 8–12 NKJV)

A REMEMBERED
CONVERSATION

If I die, keep the covenant friendship with my
family.... Stay loyal to Jonathan!
1 Samuel 20:14–15 (MSG)

Inspired by 1 Samuel 20; 2 Samuel 9

Did you ever have a conversation from your distant past come back to
you out of the blue?

Maybe it was a promise you made to someone—or someone made
to you. Maybe you'd given your word to a child, but now the years
have passed and you realize you never followed through. Or maybe it
was a promise you had whispered to the Lord in a time of sorrow or
great trial, and the Holy Spirit brought it back to your memory.

Maybe you prayed, *Lord, if You get me through this—if You help
me now and send a miracle—I will do whatever You ask me to do.*

In 2 Samuel 9, David was having such a moment.

He was remembering a conversation he'd had with his best and
dearest friend in the whole world. And he had made a promise—a

solemn promise in the Lord's name. Ironically, he had made it to Prince Jonathan, the son of David's most bitter enemy.

After all those years of running and hiding and war and fear, David was finally king over all Israel, and as the saying goes, everything seemed to be coming up roses. Scripture says:

> And David became famous after he returned from striking down eighteen thousand Edomites in the Valley of Salt....
>
> All the Edomites became subject to David. The LORD gave David victory wherever he went.
>
> David reigned over all Israel, doing what was just and right for all his people ... and David's sons were priests. (2 Sam. 8:13–15, 18 NIV).

So the Lord had given him and Israel peace and prosperity on all sides. Yet David, strangely, wasn't completely at peace himself. He couldn't forget about that intense, emotional conversation from years before. Maybe he could still see it in his mind's eye. He and the prince had been standing in a field. David was afraid for his life, and Jonathan was deeply grieved over his father's jealousy and hatred. Looking David in the eye, Jonathan had said,

> May the LORD be with you as he used to be with my father. And may you treat me with the faithful love of the LORD as long as I live. But if I die, treat my family with this faithful love, even when the LORD

destroys all your enemies from the face of the earth.
(1 Sam. 20:13–15)

Through no fault of Jonathan, his dad went completely off the rails and rebelled against the Lord, and God had plucked young David out of a sheep pasture to be the next king. Now, years later, David asked his advisers, "Is anyone in Saul's family still alive—anyone to whom I can show kindness for Jonathan's sake?" (2 Sam. 9:1).

There must have been a few raised eyebrows over that request. It went completely against the grain of the culture of that day. Normally, a new king would eliminate any potential rivals to the throne. They would have expected David to say, "Is anyone in Saul's family still alive—so I can kill them and get them out of my way?" But here was David, wanting to show kindness to Saul's family.

This word *kindness* could also be translated "grace." David is saying, "Who can I show grace to for Jonathan's sake?" What is grace? Grace is the unmerited favor of God. I'm reminded of one of the greatest statements in the whole Bible. Ephesians 2:8–9 says, "For by grace you have been saved through faith, and that not of yourselves; it is the gift of God, not of works, lest anyone should boast" (NKJV).

Let me contrast grace with mercy and justice. Justice is getting what you deserve. Mercy is *not* getting what you deserve. Grace is getting what you don't deserve at all!

Let's say that a friend borrowed my beautiful Harley and then totaled it. If I dealt with this friend in *justice*, I would say, "Okay, you need to replace my bike." If I dealt with him in *mercy*, I'd say, "Forget about it. You don't have to replace my bike." But if I dealt with him in grace, I would say, "Hey, no problem. In fact, I'm going to buy you your own bike."

This is what God has extended toward us. Because of Christ's sacrifice for us, God not only holds back the just punishment we deserve, but He gives us overwhelming, unmerited favor, opening the door of Heaven to us and calling us His own sons and daughters. The Bible goes so far as to call us "members of his household" (Eph. 2:19 NIV)!

As it turned out, Jonathan had a son, a boy who had been injured and semi-paralyzed when he was just five. His name was Mephibosheth, and nothing much had gone his way in life.

If Saul had followed the Lord and remained king, Jonathan would have been king after him and Mephibosheth next in line for the throne. But on the day his dad and grandfather were killed in battle, Mephibosheth's nurse panicked, tried to run with the boy, and accidentally dropped him. From that time on, the little prince couldn't walk.

There are people we know who have been "dropped" in life—injured by circumstances through no fault of their own. Are you one of them? Maybe some bad things happened in your childhood. Maybe there was abuse or a heartbreaking divorce. Events took place that, to this day, don't seem fair—especially when compared to the lives of others.

So you were dropped. Maybe you were mistreated, neglected, abused, and forgotten, and you haven't been given much hope. But God specializes in taking people who have been dropped in life and picking them up again.

I can imagine Mephibosheth might have been angry at David as he grew up, perhaps blaming him for all the trouble in his life. He was also afraid of David, wondering if there would come a day when David's soldiers would knock down his door and run him through with a sword.

Mephibosheth lived with a caretaker in a sad hole-in-the-wall place called Lo-Debar, a remote town in Gilead, on the east side of the Jordan. It wasn't a place that showed up in the tourist brochures. The name Lo-Debar means "no pasture." In today's world, it would be like a wide spot in the road with no stoplight and no gas station. So basically, the former prince of Israel was living in an obscure barren field in the middle of nowhere.

That's a picture of each of us before we were united with Christ. We were low. We were unloved, unwanted, and undeserving. Much of the time, we felt unneeded. But David reached out to Mephibosheth just as surely as God reached out to us. Look at 2 Samuel 9:5–6:

> David sent for him and brought him from Makir's home…. When he came to David, he bowed low to the ground in deep respect. David said, "Greetings, Mephibosheth."

Mephibosheth, who had been deathly afraid of David for as long as he could remember, found to his amazement that the king wanted to honor him, not hurt him. The Bible passage goes on to say that "from that time on, Mephibosheth ate regularly at David's table, like one of the king's own sons" (9:11).

The Bible uses this very picture to describe our relationship with the Lord. Mephibosheth ate at the king's table as though he were a member of the royal household, because he was.

David gives us a beautiful picture of Jesus in the way he deals with this situation. Remembering his promise and out of love for his friend, David demonstrated true grace to his friend's son, who had nothing to offer and could not repay him.

In the same way, God shows His deep, abiding love, though there's nothing we do to merit or deserve it. He seeks us out, calling us to His table. Mephibosheth had nothing, deserved nothing, could repay nothing. In fact, he had been dreading the king and hiding from him.

That's also a picture of us. We don't deserve His kindness. We don't merit His forgiveness. Maybe we had a false concept of God and hid from Him for years.

But what did He do? He sought us out, brought us to Himself and honored us. And someday, we will sit at a table with angels and great saints of days gone by and enjoy a meal together as His very own sons and daughters.

That isn't justice, and it is way beyond mercy.

It's nothing but pure grace.

A PAGE TORN FROM DAVID'S JOURNAL

Let all that I am praise the LORD;
    with my whole heart, I will praise his holy name.
Let all that I am praise the LORD;
    may I never forget the good things he does for me.
He forgives all my sins
    and heals all my diseases.

He redeems me from death
and crowns me with love and tender mercies.
He fills my life with good things.
My youth is renewed like the eagle's! ...

He does not punish us for all our sins;
he does not deal harshly with us, as we deserve.
For his unfailing love toward those who fear him
is as great as the height of the heavens above the
earth.
He has removed our sins as far from us
as the east is from the west.
The LORD is like a father to his children,
tender and compassionate to those who fear him.
For he knows how weak we are;
he remembers we are only dust.

(Ps. 103:1–5, 10–14)

WHEN GOD SAYS NO

Everyone will share the story of your wonderful goodness;
they will sing with joy about your righteousness.

Psalm 145:7

Inspired by 1 Chronicles 28; Psalm 145; Acts 13:36

I was having dinner with my family last week when my little grandson, Christopher, turned to me and asked, "Papa, will you remember me tomorrow?"

I looked at him, thinking, *Where did this come from?* I said, "Of course I will remember you tomorrow."

And then he said, "Papa, will you remember me one week from now?"

"Of course I'll remember you a week from now, Christopher."

"Will you remember me one month from now?"

"You know that I will! Yes, I *will* remember you one month from now."

Then he said, "Knock, knock."

I responded, "Who's there?"

He said, "I thought you said you would remember me!"

That's pretty clever. Christopher wasn't really concerned if his papa would remember him—he just wanted to put one over on him. Which he did.

In 1 Chronicles 28, we read that King David—now an old man—was ready to pass the baton to his young son, Solomon. And he was very concerned about memory. Not his own memory, but Solomon's.

Rising to his feet in front of his military leaders and royal officials, he was about to hand over the keys of the kingdom, giving Solomon leadership over the house of David. But there were some very important things he wanted his son, the new king, to remember.

> Solomon, my son, learn to know the God of your ancestors intimately. Worship and serve him with your whole heart and a willing mind. For the LORD sees every heart and knows every plan and thought. If you seek him, you will find him. But if you forsake him, he will reject you forever. So take this seriously. The LORD has chosen you to build a Temple as his sanctuary. Be strong, and do the work. (1 Chron. 28:9–10)

David had done his job. He had completed the task God had set before him. In Acts 13:36, we read these amazing words: "Now when David had served God's purpose in his own generation, he fell asleep; he was buried with his ancestors" (NIV).

This phrase *fell asleep* of course means that he died. In the New Testament, this expression is used only to describe the death of believers, never that of non-Christians. I love that picture. *Fell asleep.* I don't know about you, but for me, happy hour is a nap!

But in this context, it means that David died. But what did he do before he "fell asleep"? The Scripture says that he "served God's purpose in his own generation." What a beautiful and concise statement that is! It shows what our objective should be as Christians. When we finally "fall asleep," when we die and pass from this world, will we have completed the tasks God set before us? Will we have served the purposes of God?

What is your purpose in life? I think for some people it's just achieving a long life—which isn't a bad thing to aspire to. And if you eat enough kale and quinoa and veggie burgers, maybe you'll pull it off. But "long life" is not the objective. *Fulfilling God's purpose for your life is the objective.* Life is not measured by duration but by donation. What have you donated? What have you done with your life?

There has to come a moment when we pass from money to meaning, from possessions to purpose, from success to significance. Ultimate success is serving the purpose of God in our generation.

David had cherished a big dream for a long, long time. He wanted to build a house for the Lord, a magnificent temple. Up to this point, the Israelites had a tent set up, also called the tabernacle, where they kept the ark of the covenant. But David had a burning desire to build a permanent dwelling place for the God he loved. So he'd been saving up all his money, treasures, gold, jewels, and building supplies to accomplish that task.

But after all was prepared, the Lord told him clearly this wasn't going to happen. The Lord would not let him do what he wanted to do. Here is how David told the story.

> David rose to his feet and said: "My brothers and my
> people! It was my desire to build a Temple where the
> Ark of the LORD's Covenant, God's footstool, could
> rest permanently. I made the necessary preparations
> for building it, but God said to me, 'You must not
> build a Temple to honor my name, for you are a war-
> rior and have shed much blood.'" (1 Chron. 28:2–3)

That wasn't what David had wanted to hear from the Lord. Not at all! And sometimes it is the same for us. We pray, and yes, God answers our prayers. But we don't always get the answer we were hoping for. He doesn't always say yes. Sometimes God says "wait," and sometimes He says no.

We don't usually like it when God says no. In our hearts we keep asking, *God, why?* But He won't always tell us why—at least on this side of Heaven. We may never fully understand why He says no at certain crossroads in our lives, but we *can* know that He loves us with an everlasting love and that He has His reasons.

Maybe God has said no to you at some point in your life. You had certain dreams that didn't come about. You dreamed of a successful ministry, and it didn't happen. You dreamed of breaking new ground in your business, and that didn't happen either. Maybe you had hoped for romance and marriage, but it never came about. And perhaps at times you feel like God has let you down.

But look what David does here. Facing a no from Heaven to his most cherished ambition, David refuses to cry and moan about. He doesn't get bitter or slip into depression. Instead of crying over it, David wisely pivots to what God had done for him.

In 1 Chronicles 28:4–5, David says:

> Yet the LORD, the God of Israel, has chosen me from
> among all my father's family to be king over Israel
> forever. For he has chosen the tribe of Judah to rule,
> and from among the families of Judah he chose my
> father's family. And from among my father's sons the
> LORD was pleased to make me king over all Israel.
> And from among my sons—for the LORD has given
> me many—he chose Solomon to succeed me on the
> throne of Israel and to rule over the LORD's kingdom.

What is David saying here? "Listen, guys, I want to talk about
what God has done for me! Not just what He didn't do that I'd
wanted Him to." In other words, focus on what God has given you,
not on what He held back from you. Focus on what He *has* done for
you, not on all those things you *wish* He had done for you.

Have you been blessed by God? Has He walked with you through
life and met your needs and desires again and again and again? Has
He won a home in Heaven for you by sacrificing Himself on the cross
for you? Think about those things. Praise and thank Him for those
things. Don't let your heart become distracted, disappointed, or
embittered by what didn't happen in your life.

And remember, it is also possible that you will look back later in
life and say, "Thank You, Lord, for saying no to me on that occasion.
Thank You for keeping me from heading down that road!"

Rather than grieving over a closed door, David immediately
reflected on all God had done for him. "He chose me," David was

saying. "I was just a little shepherd kid watching a bunch of sheep. And the Lord chose me and made me the king over all Israel. How amazing! How good He has been to me!"

So focus on what God has given you, not on what He didn't give you.

In fact, He gave you Himself. And that is everything.

A PAGE TORN FROM DAVID'S JOURNAL

> I will exalt you, my God and King,
>> and praise your name forever and ever.
> I will praise you every day;
>> yes, I will praise you forever.
> Great is the LORD! He is most worthy of praise!
>> No one can measure his greatness.
>
> Let each generation tell its children of your mighty
>>> acts;
>> let them proclaim your power.
> I will meditate on your majestic, glorious splendor
>> and your wonderful miracles.
> Your awe-inspiring deeds will be on every tongue;
>> I will proclaim your greatness.
> Everyone will share the story of your wonderful
>>> goodness;
>> they will sing with joy about your righteousness.

(Ps. 145:1–7)

— DAY 20 —

OUR FUTURE IN HIS HANDS

I know, LORD, that our lives are not our own.
We are not able to plan our own course.

Jeremiah 10:23

Inspired by Psalm 31

Have you ever wondered how long you will live?

Moses wrote: "Our days may come to seventy years, or eighty, if our strength endures" (Ps. 90:10 NIV). He goes on to give some good advice, saying to the Lord:

> Teach us to number our days,
>   that we may gain a heart of wisdom.
>   (Ps. 90:12 NIV)

The fact is that Moses overshot the 70-to-80-year lifespan by quite a bit. The Lord took him home from Mount Nebo at the age of 120. But here's the question: How do we number our days when we don't know how many there will be? I think Moses might be saying, "Remember, life is short, so make the most of your time while you're walking on earth."

I read an article the other day that said AI (artificial intelligence) can now tell us—with some degree of accuracy—how long we will actually live.[1] These robot brains take into account your medical history, your location, your working hours, and a bunch of other personal details.

Then, I suppose, you can get a printout telling you how long you've got.

As far as I'm concerned, they can keep that printout. I'm not so sure I'd want to know how long I have to live. I think I like leaving that in God's hands, as David did.

Not long ago, I read about a middle-aged millionaire who was diligently trying to extend his life. At the time of the article, he was 45 years old. For the last number of years, he'd been spending two million dollars a year on anti-aging regimens. He followed a strict diet, sleep wind-down rituals, an exercise regimen, and a round of daily supplements. He underwent countless medical tests with the goal of getting his biological age down to 18. He believes death is optional, appearing to say that the length of his life is not up to God but up to *him*.[2]

Okay, we'll see how that works out. (Just don't step in front of a moving bus.)

The Bible says that "it is appointed unto men once to die, but after this the judgment" (Heb. 9:27 KJV). God has an appointed day for our birth and death, and we have everything to do with that little dash in the middle.

Some people, of course, break all the rules. Pearl Cantrell had eight children and made it to the ripe old age of 105. In an interview, she was asked how she had managed to live so long. "Hard work and bacon," she said. "I love bacon. I eat it every day."[3] I like this lady!

On another news program, interviewers asked a man who had lived past 100 for the secret of his longevity. He answered, "I eat a hot dog every day." No, I'm not advocating an unhealthy diet or habits, but ultimately, it's all in the hands of God. God determines the number of your days. And when it's your time … it's your time.

In Psalm 31:14–15, David wrote:

> I trust in you, LORD;
>> I say, "You are my God."
> My times are in your hands. (NIV)

The New Living Translation renders that last line as "My future is in your hands."

But let's put this in context. David didn't write these words lying on some beach sipping a glass of iced tea. No, he wrote this when he was on the run. Psalm 31 emerged from his lean, mean fugitive years. King Saul, in his insane jealousy of David, became obsessed with destroying the young son of Jesse.

Those weren't easy years. David was probably feeling a little nostalgic for the days when he wrestled lions and bears out in the sheep pasture. Even the fight with Goliath had been a straight-up, face-to-face battle. But now he was running and hiding, constantly looking in his rearview mirror and listening for suspicious sounds in the night.

As he told Jonathan, "I swear to you that I am only a step away from death!" (1 Sam. 20:3). In other words, he literally didn't know if his next day would be his last.

But God knew. And David told Him, "My times are in Your hands." Another version says, "Desperate, I throw myself on you: you are my God! Hour by hour I place my days in your hand" (Ps. 31:14–15 MSG).

We know that David would go on to become king—and not just king but the greatest king in the history of Israel. There's a folk song that's still popular in Israel today that little children learn at summer camps. It says, "*Dovid, melech Yisrael, chai vikayam,*" which means "David, king of Israel, lives forever."[4] That's pretty amazing to be celebrating the life of one man after three thousand years. But the most significant thing about David is that he would be in the royal line of the Messiah, and, in fact, Jesus Christ would identify Himself as the Son of David.

We know those things. But David *didn't* know those things. All he knew was that his face was on wanted posters in every post office across Israel.

Listen to this paraphrase of David's heart cry in Psalm 31:

> Be kind to me, GOD—
>   I'm in deep, deep trouble again.
> I've cried my eyes out;
>   I feel hollow inside.
> My life leaks away, groan by groan;
>   my years fade out in sighs.

My troubles have worn me out,
    turned my bones to powder.
To my enemies I'm a monster;
    I'm ridiculed by the neighbors.
My friends are horrified;
    they cross the street to avoid me.
They want to blot me from memory.
       (Ps. 31:9–12 MSG)

Yet in that same psalm, perhaps with tears running down his face, he says, "You are my God. My times—my future—are in Your hand. I'm trusting You, Lord" (see vv. 14–15).

David didn't know how long he would live. He didn't know if he would ever make it to the throne. He didn't know if he would see his next birthday. But he knew his God, and he trusted Him.

The bottom line here? Stop worrying about how long you're going to live. Put away the speculations and the gloomy talk. Tell those AI programs that predict lifespan to take a hike. All the tofu and kale and green smoothies in the world will not extend your life. That's in the Lord's hands. So have a few pieces of bacon and enjoy yourself. It worked out for Pearl Cantrell, didn't it?

Jesus asked, "Which of you by being anxious can add a single hour to his span of life?" (Matt. 6:27 ESV). God has a future planned for you. We know this because the Lord said in Jeremiah 29:11, "I know the plans I have for you.... They are plans for good and not for disaster, to give you a future and a hope."

As Corrie ten Boom was known for saying, "Never be afraid to trust an unknown future to a known God."

A PAGE TORN FROM DAVID'S JOURNAL

I am trusting you, O LORD,
    saying, "You are my God!"
My future is in your hands.
    Rescue me from those who hunt me down
        relentlessly.
Let your favor shine on your servant.
    In your unfailing love, rescue me.
Don't let me be disgraced, O LORD,
    for I call out to you for help.

(Ps. 31:14–17)

THE COURAGE
TO FORGIVE

You have not handed me over to my enemies
but have set me in a safe place.

Psalm 31:8

Inspired by Psalm 31

It often comes as a surprise to us, as Christians, when we discover we're opposed not only by the world but by some fellow believers.

It just doesn't make sense to us.

Some Christian you know—or someone you've reached out to in friendship—may turn on you, criticize you, or give you the cold shoulder.

Before everything fell apart for David, he had been anointed as the future king. But then the scene changed, and the once-godly Saul was literally trying to kill him. You think *you* have in-law problems?

This is the situation David was dealing with when he wrote Psalm 31.

> Pull me from the trap my enemies set for me,
>> for I find protection in you alone.
> I entrust my spirit into your hand.
>> Rescue me, LORD, for you are a faithful God....
>
> Have mercy on me, LORD, for I am in distress.
>> Tears blur my eyes.
>> My body and soul are withering away.
> I am dying from grief;
>> my years are shortened by sadness....
> I am scorned by all my enemies
>> and despised by my neighbors—
>> even my friends are afraid to come near me.
> When they see me on the street,
>> they run the other way. (vv. 4–5, 9–11)

So David was in trouble. His neighbors wouldn't answer their doors when he knocked, and his friends wouldn't take his calls. And it all started with the jealousy of the insecure King Saul.

There is a story about a crab fisherman who'd had a successful catch and was walking along with a basketful of crabs. There was no lid on the basket, and someone said, "Hey, how do you keep those crabs in that bucket? Don't they want to climb out?" "Oh, yeah," the fisherman replied. "But there's no problem. As soon as one starts to climb up, the others reach over and pull him back down." That's jealousy. I may be on the way to the crab pot, but I'm taking you with me!

The bottom line is that people are going to hurt you. And, by the way, you will hurt people too. Sometimes, you will even be hurt by people you tried to help, and the only way you can deal with the fallout is to keep short accounts and forgive them.

Even if they don't deserve your forgiveness, forgive them anyway. It will help you sleep better at night. Max Lucado wrote: "God allows us to feel the frailty of human love so we'll appreciate the strength of his love."[1]

We live in a culture that does not value forgiveness. In fact, forgiveness is seen as a sign of weakness. Our culture values vengeance and payback. (Think of all the revenge-themed movies out there!) Many operate by the old adage "I don't get mad; I get even." And then they end up drinking the poison that was meant for someone else.

Forgiveness doesn't mean condoning or dismissing bad behavior. It doesn't even necessarily suggest reconciliation. It just means you forgive. "But wait," you say, "shouldn't we be reconciled to people?"

Yes, if it's possible. But it isn't always possible.

I love the way the apostle Paul put it to the Christians in Rome: "If it is possible, as far as it depends on you, live at peace with everyone" (Rom. 12:18 NIV). Some people simply don't want peace. They want to stay offended, stay angry. If that's the case, pray that God will change their hearts. But don't let it steal your joy.

When you can't reconcile with someone, you can still forgive them. You don't need their cooperation for that to happen. And there is nothing they can do to stop you. If for nothing else, forgive them for your own peace of mind. Surrender the right to "get even" and to "give them what they deserve."

But I'm not saying it will be easy.

Listen to David's anguish as he describes the betrayal of a close friend:

> It was not an enemy who taunted me—then I could have borne it; I could have hidden and escaped. But it was you, a man like myself, my companion and my friend. What fellowship we had, what wonderful discussions as we walked together to the Temple of the Lord on holy days....
>
> This friend of mine betrayed me—I who was at peace with him. He broke his promises. (Ps. 55:12–14, 20 TLB)

But David learned to forgive. And that's another reason that he was a man after God's own heart. He had multiple opportunities to kill Saul, but he refused to raise his hand against him. As we saw earlier, he even extended incredible grace to Saul's grandson, giving him a permanent place at the king's table.

Sometimes you will hear people say, "I'm mad at the church. I've had it with them. The church hurt me." What they mean is that they went to a particular local church and had a bad experience. So now they're angry at the entire church of Jesus around the entire world?

That would be like saying, "I went to a restaurant and had a bad meal, so now I will never eat in a restaurant again!" That probably won't happen. Or maybe, "I didn't like the way that doctor treated me, so I'm done with doctors. I'll never go back."

Just remember this: It was the Lord Jesus Christ who established His church, and one day you will need the church very much—even more than you realize.

There was a popular song in Israel, right after David killed Goliath, an event that turned the tide of battle for God's people and crushed their enemies. It was actually a dance number. The women sang it in the streets while dancing with tambourines: "Saul has slain his thousands, and David his tens of thousands" (1 Sam. 29:5 NIV). In modern terms, this song was number one on a streaming music service. Even the Philistines knew the words and probably caught themselves humming the tune.

But think of all the grief, sorrow, loss of productivity, and long, wasted years that could have been avoided if Saul had said, "Oh, well. I guess the kid deserves the praise. That was a pretty gutsy move. Good for him! Great to have him on the team."

But that's not what happened. A hellish shadow of jealousy fell over the king's heart *and never left*. In other words, Saul's obsession with David's "offense" defined the rest of his life, colored the rest of his days, and even opened the door to demonic activity in his soul.

It's a story as old as Cain and Abel in the fourth chapter of Genesis. Abel got commended for his sacrifice to the Lord, but the offering of his brother Cain didn't measure up. Because of Cain's jealousy, we have the first examples of anger and depression in human history.

And the first murder. Cain's angry and offended spirit defined the rest of his life, and there was no going back.

Don't let that happen. Don't let someone else's action or sin or selfishness define the rest of your life. Don't let today's offense become tomorrow's stumbling block.

David refused to let that happen. In Psalm 55:22, immediately after pouring out his heart to God about the close friend who had turned on him, David wrote these words:

> Give your burdens to the LORD,
>   and he will take care of you.
>   He will not permit the godly to slip and fall.

David had been hurt, betrayed, and offended. But he didn't let that define his life.

He let the Lord do that.

A PAGE TORN FROM DAVID'S JOURNAL

> I waited patiently for the LORD's help;
>   then he listened to me and heard my cry.
> He pulled me out of a dangerous pit,
>   out of the deadly quicksand.
> He set me safely on a rock
>   and made me secure.
> He taught me to sing a new song,
>   a song of praise to our God.
> Many who see this will take warning
>   and will put their trust in the LORD....

May all who come to you
   be glad and joyful.
May all who are thankful for your salvation
   always say, "How great is the LORD!"

I am weak and poor, O Lord
   but you have not forgotten me.
You are my savior and my God—
   hurry to my aid!

(Ps. 40:1–3, 16–17 GNT)

Hope in the Lord

*You have not given me into the hands of the enemy
but have set my feet in a spacious place.*

Psalm 31:8 (NIV)

Inspired by Psalm 31

Where is your hope right now? Is your hope in money? Is your hope in your career? Is your hope in your family—as wonderful as that family might be? Is your hope in a politician or political party? All these will let you down in some way, shape, or form.

So will Christian leaders. Your pastor may be a top-notch guy, but he will inevitably disappoint you. At some point, he will be distracted by a thousand little fires breaking out here and there, and he may miss the desperate note in your call for help.

Your dearest friends won't always come through for you. It may not be intentional, but they have their own set of pressing issues, and they may neglect to return your text or call. A friend of mine told me about how his wife's two best friends began to avoid her when she had a terminal illness. They couldn't bear to see her suffer, so they stopped coming around—just when she needed them most.

Your health will fail you. When you are right in the middle of your long-held plans or living your dream, a troubling health issue will pop up, putting everything else on hold.

But God will not fail you. He is never distracted. Even with a seemingly endless universe to run and a trillion galaxies swirling in space, you have His full attention. In Psalm 37:23, David wrote:

> The LORD directs the steps of the godly.
> He delights in every detail of their lives.

Wow! *Every detail.* And on top of that, He never misses calls. You won't be sent to voicemail or an operator overseas. The Lord told Jeremiah: "Call to Me, and I will answer you, and show you great and mighty things, which you do not know" (Jer. 33:3 NKJV). The prophet may not have received all the answers he longed for, but God walked with him through even the darkest days. He would later write: "*His compassion never ends.* It is only the Lord's mercies that have kept us from complete destruction. Great is his faithfulness; his loving-kindness begins afresh each day" (Lam. 3:22–23 TLB).

You might say that all David's hopes—the things he used to ponder out under the stars with his sheep—had been completely crushed. He had lost hope in his friends, in the government of Israel, and in the normal desires for a home and family life. You can't have those things if you've been branded as a dangerous outlaw.

But he never lost hope in the Lord.

In Psalm 31 he wrote:

> Oh, love the LORD, all you His saints!
> For the LORD preserves the faithful,
> And fully repays the proud person.
> Be of good courage,
> And He shall strengthen your heart,
> All you who hope in the LORD. (vv. 23–24 NKJV)

Psalm 119:114 says, "You are my refuge and my shield, and your promises are my only source of hope" (TLB). Did you pick up on that? The psalmist's hope does not consist of the promises of God *and* his 401(k) ... *and* his last great physical ... *and* his success on the job. Those are all blessings to be thankful for, but David knew that his only enduring hope was in the Lord Himself.

In Romans 15:4, Paul reminds us: "Such things were written in the Scriptures long ago to teach us. And the Scriptures give us hope and encouragement as we wait patiently for God's promises to be fulfilled."

We need hope in this life. Without it, we will never find rest and peace.

Corrie ten Boom said, "If you look at the world, you'll be distressed. If you look within, you'll be depressed. But if you look at Christ, you'll be at rest."[1]

Again, David wrote Psalms 27 and 31 when all his earthly plans and dreams were up in the air. Even so, he could still scratch these words out on a scroll: "Wait on the LORD; be of good courage, and He shall strengthen your heart; wait, I say, on the LORD!" (Ps. 27:14 NKJV).

Does it take courage to put your hope in God and wait on Him—even when you're not seeing any change or immediate results? Yes, it does. I think it took David just as much courage to hope in and wait on God as it did to grab a lion by the jaw or run to the battle line to face a giant. You see, David didn't know the rest of his story; he didn't know what would happen in the days and years to come. And neither do we. We don't know the rest of our story, do we?

But that's okay, because we aren't writing it!

He is writing our story. Sometimes He may put a comma where we would like a period or a period where we would like a comma. Sometimes He might end a much-loved chapter way too soon, and at other times He allows a difficult chapter to continue on.

But He is "the author and finisher of our faith" (Heb. 12:2 NKJV). He's writing your story. If you are walking with Him through your days, you can count on it being a *good* story. And when you get to the end of it, you will look back and say, "Lord, thank You that You were in control of my life."

In what or in whom is your hope today? Will that hope sustain you in your last hour? Only God can do that for you. Here's the good news: As a Christian, I am indestructible until God is done with me. But when His task for me is done, that's it. He calls me home.

I don't decide the length of my life through all my health regimens and vitamin supplements. Maybe I will enjoy a healthier life, but that's in the hands of God. Until the Lord is done, I don't have to worry about any threat against my life.

When the apostle Paul was stoned, bloodied, and left for dead by the mob in Lystra, the Bible says that "after the disciples had gathered around him, he got up and went back into the city" (Acts 14:20 NIV).

The stoning was supposed to have killed him. Maybe it should have killed him. But he walked away from it and went back to work. Why? Because it wasn't his time.

When Paul was shipwrecked on the island of Malta, he was building a fire on the beach when a highly venomous viper bit him on the hand. What did Paul do? He shook it off into the fire and went on gathering driftwood (see Acts 28:3–5).

Again, it wasn't his time.

But then the day came when the Roman executioner walked into Paul's prison cell and led him to the chopping block. When he was executed, he went instantly to Heaven because it finally was his time. Until that moment came, he was extremely productive, writing the book of 2 Timothy just before his death—a book that has been changing lives all over the world for twenty centuries.

God wants us to focus on today. Every day is His gift to us. Every day is a treasure beyond calculation. Live it for His glory. Stop checking in every day with all your worries and fears, and instead focus on living your life to the fullest for the glory of God. See every day for what it truly is.

It's a gift. It's a treasure. Don't waste it.

A PAGE TORN FROM DAVID'S JOURNAL

I wait quietly before God,
for my victory comes from him.

He alone is my rock and my salvation,
    my fortress where I will never be shaken....

Let all that I am wait quietly before God,
    for my hope is in him.
He alone is my rock and my salvation,
    my fortress where I will not be shaken.
My victory and honor come from God alone.
    He is my refuge, a rock where no enemy can
        reach me.
O my people, trust in him at all times.
    Pour out your heart to him,
    for God is our refuge.

(Ps. 62:1–2, 5–8)

THE GOD WHO KNOWS EVERYTHING

I'm an open book to you;
even from a distance, you know what I'm thinking.

Psalm 139:2 (MSG)

Inspired by Psalm 139

There are only so many things you can explain to a baby.

When our granddaughter Stella was two, I would try to show her or teach her a few things. But, smart as she was, her comprehension went only so far. I might use an object or draw a picture to help her understand, and maybe that would help her grasp a little of what I was saying.

But back when she was still a little baby, she didn't understand my words at all. She saw my facial expressions and heard the inflection in my voice, and we had a great time smiling and cooing at each other.

But how could I explain a concept to her? How could I explain Hawaii to a baby? I might say, "Stella, let me tell you about Hawaii.

It's a wonderful place, Stella. The sky is blue. The water is warm. The sand is soft. Papa loves it there."

She might like hearing about it, because she could see in my face that I was talking about something that made me light up, but she would have no idea what I was saying.

So here we are as human beings trying to grasp the nature of God, the almighty Creator and Sovereign of the universe. And we try different ways to make God fit into our minds or the structure of our thoughts. Sometimes He does, a little. But often He does not.

This isn't a cop-out or an excuse. It's just the way things are. It's reality.

It is a simple acknowledgment that I will never be able to fully comprehend God this side of Heaven. And even on the other side, it will take an eternity for me to even scratch the surface.

It has been said, "If God were small enough for my mind, He wouldn't be big enough for my needs." In 1 Corinthians 13, Paul gives us the promise that we will have much more understanding when we are with the Lord in eternity:

> Now we see things imperfectly, like puzzling reflections in a mirror, but then we will see everything with perfect clarity. All that I know now is partial and incomplete, but then I will know everything completely, just as God now knows me completely. (v. 12)

Now, having said that we cannot fully *comprehend* God, let me clarify that we can *know* God. In fact, knowing God is the essence of being a Christian. In John 17, Jesus tells us, "This is the way to have eternal life—to know you, the only true God, and Jesus Christ, the one you sent to earth" (v. 3).

That is we why we are on earth: to know God and make Him known.

But we may still find ourselves wondering, *What is God like? Does God know literally everything? Can God be present all around the world at the same time? And does God actually care about someone like me?*

In Psalm 139, we find David, "the man after [God's] own heart" (1 Sam. 13:14 NIV), seemingly gazing up into the heavens and expressing his awe and wonder to a God he loved but barely understood:

> O Lord, you have examined my heart and know everything about me. You know when I sit or stand. When far away you know my every thought. You chart the path ahead of me and tell me where to stop and rest. Every moment you know where I am. You know what I am going to say before I even say it. You both precede and follow me and place your hand of blessing on my head. (Ps. 139:1–5 TLB)

David says, "You know what I am going to say even before I say it." Wow. *I* don't even know what I am going to say before I say it! And there have been times when I have said things I wish I hadn't. If I'd known what I was going to say before I said it, maybe I wouldn't have said it!

From this and many other verses in the Bible we learn that God's knowledge is as eternal as He is. What God knows now He has always known and will always know. Unlike you and me, God doesn't learn new things, nor does He forget what He knows.

I read a magazine article that said the human brain can store up to a million billion bits of information. That sounds like guesswork to me, but it wouldn't surprise me if it were true. We've all had the experience of being somewhere or encountering some sound or fragrance and flashing back to a scene or memory from many years ago. It's surprising how vivid those memories can be!

God, however, remembers everything. At all times. There is never a lapse in His recollections. He never forgets anyone, ever. What's more, He knows everything that transpires in every corner of His creation at every moment. He knows about a speck of red dust four yards under the surface of Mars. He has watched the sunrise on planets our most powerful telescopes have never discerned. Psalm 147:4 tells us He knows every star in the universe *by name*.

But now let's personalize it. Not only does He know all this information and data, but He also knows *you*.

Jesus said, "The very hairs of your head are all numbered" (Luke 12:7 NKJV). (Not such a big deal, perhaps, in my case.) He knows your every thought. Your every intention. Your every move, down to the beat of your heart and the blink of your eyes.

This awesome God who created the universe and numbers the stars in a trillion galaxies is actually very interested in you. This was what blew David's mind. He tried to wrap his thoughts around it, but the concept was too massive to grasp. He wrote: "This is too glorious, too wonderful to believe!" (Ps. 139:6 TLB).

Another version says, "This is too much, too wonderful—I can't take it all in!" (MSG).

What bothers you? What brings you heartache? What brings tears to your eyes? What was weighing on your mind last night as you drifted off to sleep? God is concerned with these things. You can either believe that or not, but the statement is absolutely true.

In Psalm 56:8, when David was running from the Philistines, he found time to write: "You keep track of all of my sorrows. You have collected all my tears in your bottle. You have recorded each one in your book."

Whatever you may be facing right now, the Lord knows about it. He doesn't just see you; He sees *through* you. Of course, when Jesus walked this earth, God in human form, He would read people's minds and hearts, which drove them crazy. He would say, "Why are you thinking thus and so in your heart?"

When Nathanael sat by himself under a fig tree, perhaps thinking about God, Jesus told him later, "I could see you under the fig tree before Philip found you" (John 1:48). He sensed Nathanael's hunger for God from afar.

God knows every thought we think. How preposterous to imagine we could ever hide something from Him! That is why David was in such depression and misery when he was living with unconfessed sin. He had to try to shut God out of his thoughts, but at the same time he *knew* God was displeased. He *knew* God was grieved over what he had done to the family of Uriah and Bathsheba.

After he had finally confessed the sin and had opened his heart to the Lord again, he wrote: "Behold, You desire truth in the inward

parts, and in the hidden part You will make me to know wisdom"
(Ps. 51:6 NKJV).

God knows when we have stretched the truth, coddled a lustful thought, entertained feelings of pride, or cut corners with the
way we handle money. We can't cover it up. Everything will be
made known.

What's more, He knows what will happen in my life before it
happens. Nothing catches God by surprise. He doesn't say, "Whoa!
Where did *that* come from?"

That's because God dwells in the eternal realm. In Isaiah 46:10,
He says, "Only I can tell you the future before it even happens.
Everything I plan will come to pass, for I do whatever I wish."

God knows the end from the beginning.

God has known you in the womb, and He knows the day you
will step into eternity. And He wants to walk with you, step by step,
through all your days.

Truths like that blew David's circuit breakers. He wrote:

> How precious it is, Lord, to realize that you are
> thinking about me constantly! I can't even count
> how many times a day your thoughts turn toward
> me. And when I waken in the morning, you are still
> thinking of me! (Ps. 139:17–18 TLB).

You can leave the details of your life today in His hands.
All of them.
If you don't, you are missing a blessing.

A Page Torn from David's Journal

O LORD, You have searched me and known me.
You know my sitting down and my rising up;
You understand my thought afar off.
You comprehend my path and my lying down,
And are acquainted with all my ways.
For there is not a word on my tongue,
But behold, O LORD, You know it altogether.
You have hedged me behind and before,
And laid Your hand upon me.
Such knowledge is too wonderful for me;
It is high, I cannot attain it.

(Ps. 139:1–6 NKJV)

HE IS HERE;
HE IS STRONG

If I flew on morning's wings
to the far western horizon,
You'd find me in a minute—
you're already there waiting!

Psalm 139:9–10 (MSG)

Inspired by Psalm 139

David took time to reflect on the beauty and wonder and immensity of God. The Bible doesn't tell us where he was when he wrote Psalm 139. Was he in his cedar-paneled palace? It makes more sense to me that he was walking under the stars—or maybe along a beach at sunset (which is where I would want to be).

He thought about God's knowledge, how the Lord knows everything that is, that was, that will be, and even that *could* be.

And then he paused on the thought that God is everywhere. For David, who had spent so many lonely nights taking refuge in empty deserts and desolate caves, God's presence meant something incredibly valuable to him. It meant he was never alone.

Even if everyone he knew deserted him and turned away, even if his wife turned her back on him and his best friend died, he would never be on his own. The Lord God Himself would be with him. And David took great comfort from that.

In Psalm 139, he wrote:

> I can *never* be lost to your Spirit! I can *never* get away from my God! If I go up to heaven, you are there; if I go down to the place of the dead, you are there. If I ride the morning winds to the farthest oceans, even there your hand will guide me, your strength will support me. If I try to hide in the darkness, the night becomes light around me. (Ps. 139:7–11 TLB)

Those words could either be comforting or frightening, depending on which side of the fence you find yourself. If you are a follower of Jesus, they bring great comfort.

God is not bound by geographical boundaries or time zones. He is present everywhere. No matter what you may be facing or enduring right now, He is (literally, in fact) there with you. In Hebrews 13:5, we have our Lord's comforting words: "Never will I leave you; never will I forsake you" (NIV).

In Greek, the original language the New Testament was written in, that statement is very emphatic. It could better be translated, "I will never, no never, no never leave you or forsake you."

What are you going through right now? You are not alone. The omnipresent God is there walking with you through it. He says in the book of Isaiah:

When you go through deep waters,
   I will be with you.
When you go through rivers of difficulty,
   you will not drown.
When you walk through the fire of oppression,
   you will not be burned up;
   the flames will not consume you. (43:2)

Or, as David himself wrote, "Yea, though I walk through the valley of the shadow of death,... You are with me" (Ps. 23:4 NKJV).

Wherever you go, God is there. C. S. Lewis wrote: "We may ignore, but we can nowhere evade, the presence of God. The world is crowded with Him."[1]

I have a friend who had this encouraging thought: Whenever he enters a room—whether it's a classroom or a doctor's office or some new place he has never been—he reminds himself that the Lord has gone ahead of him. With this in mind, he imagines little yellow sticky notes around the room. The notes read: "I've already been here" or "I've already got this scoped out" or "I'm with you right now."

It's an incredible comfort knowing that our God is omnipresent, that He is everywhere we need Him to be. But in addition to that, He is omnipotent. That means He is all-powerful.

More specifically, *omnipotence* means God has infinite power that can never be depleted, drained, or exhausted in the slightest degree.

I remember my first iPhone. I loved it and all the novel things it could do. I carried it around with me all day. But the problem was it just wouldn't hold a charge very long. I could barely make it through a day. By about four or five o'clock in the afternoon, I could see that its battery was getting low—maybe even in the red zone. So I would have to find a place to plug it in.

It's the same for people who drive electric vehicles. *How far can I get down the road before I have to plug in my car—and what happens if I can't find a working charging station?* They call it range anxiety.

God's resources, however, are never exhausted. He doesn't have to recharge or refuel at night. His mighty strength has never been diminished in the slightest, nor will it ever be. Yes, He rested after He made the universe in seven days, but it wasn't because He was tired.

That's why it's so ridiculous when someone says, "Well, I've tried everything I can think of, so now all I can do is just"—gulp—"pray."

Well, yes.

All you can do now is call out to the omniscient, omnipresent, omnipotent Creator of the universe, who knows the name of every star, sees every sparrow that falls, keeps a running count of every hair on your head, and loves you with a love that can't be measured or imagined.

Your requirements are never a drain on God's resources. You will *never* need more than God can supply. Paul expressed this in the book of Ephesians—and seemed to almost run out of words: "Now to Him who is able to do exceedingly abundantly above all that we ask or think" (3:20 NKJV).

I like the way these words are paraphrased in *The Message* version: "God can do anything, you know—far more than you could ever imagine or guess or request in your wildest dreams!"

So consider your circumstances right now. What are you going through? What are the anxieties that seem to seep up through the floorboards? Maybe you are overwhelmed by tragedy or grief or sorrow. Maybe confusion or uncertainty has you in a fog. Then again, maybe you are bound by an addiction of some kind—one so powerful it has turned into a lifestyle—and you feel as though you will never be free from it.

Are you ready to bring it to the Lord and place it at His feet? The all-knowing, all-powerful, everywhere-present God is ready to help you.

I love the Old Testament story of King Hezekiah of Judah when he was threatened by a huge Assyrian army. The Assyrians had completely surrounded Jerusalem. Sennacherib, the arrogant king of that evil empire, sent a message to Hezekiah—an evil, threatening letter that mocked God and God's people.

Hezekiah could have sat in his throne room and had a meltdown over that letter, yelling at his servants and smashing a few vases. But he didn't. Scripture says Hezekiah got up, went to the Lord's temple, "and spread [the letter] before the LORD" (2 Kings 19:14 NKJV). He appealed to God to defend little Judah against this mighty army.

The answer came back right away. Isaiah, the Lord's prophet, told him, "Because you prayed about King Sennacherib of Assyria, the LORD has spoken this word against him" (Isa. 37:21–22).

And that night, one solitary angel of God—all by himself—went out and put to death the entire invading army.

God told Hezekiah in effect, "Because you prayed, because you brought this impossible problem to Me, believing in My power and protection, this is what I will do."

"Because you prayed."

But what if he hadn't prayed? Would the city have experienced that supernatural breakthrough? We really don't know what would have happened.

God can do what needs to be done when it needs to be done. What He is waiting for you to do is to call out to Him. Yes, He is infinite. Yes, He is powerful beyond conception.

But He is knowable. He *wants* to be known.

At times, we struggle to wrap our minds around a Supreme Being who is so beyond our understanding. But that's one reason Jesus came. If you want to know what God is like, just look at Jesus. Jesus is God. Right before He went to the cross, He told Philip, "Don't you know me, Philip, even after I have been among you such a long time? Anyone who has seen me has seen the Father" (John 14:9 NIV).

God had a face.

God wants to show His affection, His plan, His purpose, and His strong hand of help and rescue to each one of us.

Because that is what God is like.

He just loves us.

A Page Torn from David's Journal

You made all the delicate, inner parts of my body and knit them together in my mother's womb. Thank you for making me so wonderfully complex! It is amazing to think about. Your workmanship is marvelous—and how well I know it. You were there while I was being formed in utter seclusion! You saw me before I was born and scheduled each day of my life before I began to breathe. Every day was recorded in your book!

(Ps. 139:13–16 TLB)

REMEMBERING TO REMEMBER

I'll ponder all the things you've accomplished,
and give a long, loving look at your acts.

Psalm 77:12 (MSG)

Inspired by Psalm 103

Sometimes I talk to myself.

I may remind myself of something I have to do as I walk from one end of the house to the other. (It's amazing how easily distracted I can become.) I may encourage myself to walk on by the doughnut shop instead of stopping in for a visit. At other times, I will recite a Scripture—maybe one I memorized many years ago—and tell myself to pay attention to it.

It encourages me to know that David did that too. He spoke to his own soul, urging himself to remember God's goodness and help.

In Psalm 103, it sounds like this:

Bless the LORD, O my soul;
And all that is within me, bless His holy name!

Bless the LORD, O my soul,
And forget not all His benefits:
Who forgives all your iniquities,
Who heals all your diseases,
Who redeems your life from destruction,
Who crowns you with lovingkindness and tender
        mercies,
Who satisfies your mouth with good things,
So that your youth is renewed like the eagle's.
        (vv. 1–5 NKJV)

David was talking to himself—and to us too, by extension.

He was talking to his soul, his innermost being, and reminding himself to remember all the good things God had done for him. He was saying, "Come on, soul. Wake up. Remember how God forgave my sins, got me up off the sickbed, saved me from death a thousand times over?"

Really? We need reminding to bless and praise the Lord for being good to us? Well, yes, we actually do. At least David thought so. It is obvious he was afraid of taking all God's goodness and blessings for granted.

We see this call to remembrance again in Psalm 42. The writer speaks to his own soul, trying to jog his own memory:

Take courage, my soul! Do you remember those
times (but how could you ever forget them!) when
you led a great procession to the Temple on festival
days, singing with joy, praising the Lord? Why then

be downcast? Why be discouraged and sad? Hope
in God! (Ps. 42:4–5 TLB)

Talking to yourself, then, isn't necessarily bad—as long as you
say the right things! And reminding ourselves to remember God, His
provision, and His goodness is one of the most important things we
could do.

In Psalm 77, the psalmist makes this pledge:

> I will remember the deeds of the LORD;
>   yes, I will remember your miracles of long ago.
> I will consider all your works
>   and meditate on all your mighty deeds.
>   (Ps. 77:11–12 NIV)

Remembering is always an issue. I have noticed that as I get older
(and I am certainly getting older), I am forgetting things more and
more.

There have been times I've been looking for my reading glasses,
only to find them already on my head. That's a little embarrassing.
Nevertheless, I seem to spend more time these days looking for items
I have misplaced.

The experts tell us to put important items back in special, desig-
nated places so we will always know where to look. But what if you
forget where those special places are?

There are times I forget where I parked my car. If I'm in a parking
structure, I can't remember if my car is on level one, two, three, or
four. So I walk around with my little key fob, pushing the button

and hoping the car alarm will sound. I don't like doing that, but then I look around and see other people doing the same thing, so I feel a little better.

The bottom line is that I need reminders.

Sometimes, in addition to talking to myself, I will jot notes to myself. I may even ask someone, "Hey, would you remind me to do thus and so this afternoon?"

There are also reminder items we carry with us. On my finger, for instance, I have a ring to remind me I am married. But I don't really need the ring to remind me, because there is a woman who has lived in my house for fifty years who is only too happy to remind me.

In church we observe the Communion table as a reminder. That's why the Lord gave it to us. Luke tells us that at the Last Supper, Jesus "took some bread and gave thanks to God for it. Then he broke it in pieces and gave it to the disciples, saying, 'This is my body, which is given for you. *Do this in remembrance of me*'" (Luke 22:19).

Do we really need to set aside a time in a church service—and do we really need little crackers and grape juice—to remember what Jesus did for us on the cross? Apparently, we do. We need reminding. Why? Because we forget things! Even important things.

The Bible is filled with repetition. It tells us the same things over and over and over again. Why is that? Because we are so forgetful. What I have found is that I tend to remember what I ought to forget and forget what I ought to remember.

Why is my mind still filled with pointless trivia I have no use for whatsoever? I can't get rid of it no matter how hard I try. I think to myself, *Did I consciously memorize the lyrics to stupid commercials and songs I never liked from the beginning? And how is it I can't remember Bible verses I've actually committed to memory?*

So I find myself doing what David did: I remind myself to remember. I try to refresh my memory of the most important things over and over again.

David said, "May I never forget the good things he does for me" (Ps. 103:2).

The apostle Peter agrees: "I plan to keep on reminding you of these things even though you already know them" (2 Pet. 1:12 TLB). In other words, "You may get tired of these reminders, but that's okay. I'm going to keep reminding you."

We need to remember and focus on what God has said about Himself. What you think about God has everything to do with how you live your life. Your view of God will determine how you react to what comes your way on any given day.

Maybe you have been wrestling with some oversized worries. Maybe you have been feeling as though you are all alone—adrift at sea with no one to help. In the lowest of these moments, maybe you wonder if God has abandoned you or is busy with other people He loves more.

Nothing could be further from the truth.

God is here with you right now. At this moment, I am the one reminding you of that. But there is another who will also jog your memory. He is the Holy Spirit. As He was getting ready to leave this earth, Jesus told His distraught disciples, "When the Father sends the Advocate as my representative—that is, the Holy Spirit—he will teach you everything and will remind you of everything I have told you" (John 14:26).

It's the Holy Spirit who whispers encouragement when we're feeling lost or lonely or weighed down with worries. And the more Scripture you've put into your mind, the more He will have to work with when the hard times come—or when the bottom falls out of your life.

Paul wrote to the Corinthian church that the Lord "comes alongside us when we go through hard times, and before you know it, he brings us alongside someone else who is going through hard times so that we can be there for that person just as God was there for us" (2 Cor. 1:4 MSG).

That's a wonderful promise!

Let's remind each other to remember it.

A Page Torn from David's Journal

Give thanks to the LORD and proclaim his
    greatness.
  Let the whole world know what he has done.
Sing to him; yes, sing his praises.
  Tell everyone about his wonderful deeds.
Exult in his holy name;
  rejoice, you who worship the LORD.
Search for the LORD and for his strength;
  continually seek him.
Remember the wonders he has performed,
  his miracles, and the rulings he has given.

(Ps. 105:1–5)

THE GOD WHO RESTORES

He restores my soul.

Psalm 23:3 (NKJV)

Inspired by Psalm 23

A careless sheep may occasionally find itself in a terrible dilemma. It's called being "cast" or "cast down."

It's when a sheep gets stuck on its back—somewhat like a tortoise. So the little woolly is out there grazing and maybe decides to lie on its side for a while. But then it accidentally rolls down a slope or slips into a ravine. Once on its back, it can't right itself. If the shepherd doesn't search for that animal and get it back on its four legs within twenty-four hours, the sheep will die.

The late W. Phillip Keller, who was a shepherd himself, wrote: "A cast sheep is a very pathetic sight. Lying on its back, its feet in the air, it flays away frantically struggling to stand up, without success. Sometimes it will bleat a little for help, but generally it lies there lashing about in frightened frustration."[1]

There is no button for the sheep to push, like on the old commercials when someone says, "I've fallen, and I can't get up."

It takes a shepherd to restore a cast-down sheep.

Our Shepherd is our restorer. David, who knew all about the peculiarities of sheep, wrote: "He makes me lie down in green pastures, he leads me beside quiet waters, he refreshes my soul" (Ps. 23:2–3 NIV).

Our Shepherd searches us out and picks us up when we fall into the ravines of life. He restores and revives us. He gets us back on our feet again. He infuses us with new strength. Another version of Psalm 23:3 says: "True to your word, you let me catch my breath and send me in the right direction" (MSG).

Sheep, weak and defenseless as they are, get themselves into all kinds of trouble. Sometimes they go astray. And a sheep that becomes separated from the shepherd and flock may quickly end up as fast food for a predator.

David spoke about sheep, but so did the Son of David. Jesus told the story about a secure flock of one hundred sheep—and the one that went rogue.

> If a man has a hundred sheep and one of them gets
> lost, what will he do? Won't he leave the ninety-nine
> others in the wilderness and go to search for the one
> that is lost until he finds it? And when he has found
> it, he will joyfully carry it home on his shoulders.
> When he arrives, he will call together his friends
> and neighbors, saying, "Rejoice with me because I
> have found my lost sheep." (Luke 15:4–6)

Jesus' story gives an example of another meaning of *restore*: to find something that has been lost. In case His disciples needed another illustration (and they usually did), Jesus told them about a woman who had ten silver coins but lost one somewhere in her house. Anxious and distressed, she swept every corner of her home, looking for it (see Luke 15:8–10).

This wasn't a casual search for something trivial, like looking for a dime in the shag carpet. This coin was extremely valuable to her. The brides of this time would wear a piece of jewelry with ten silver coins on it. So our modern equivalent would be like a bride losing her wedding ring.

When she finally found it, she was so overcome with joy that she threw a party. Jesus said, "She will call in her friends and neighbors and say, 'Rejoice with me because I have found my lost coin'" (Luke 15:9).

It's an amazing feeling to lose something—imagining it is totally gone—and then find it days, weeks, or even years later.

I read about a lady who had a favorite book go missing. Years later, she saw a used copy of the same book online and ordered it—only to discover that it was the very book she had lost. Another man lost his iPhone in early February and then found it in March, frozen in a snowdrift near the driveway. And it still worked! An elderly man lost his gold wedding ring while working in the garden. Weeks later, when he was harvesting some of his vegetables, he found the ring literally embedded in a carrot.[2]

The Lord is all about finding lost things ... and restoring broken things.

In the pages of the book of Job, we read about a man who found himself suddenly buried in an avalanche of tragedy and loss, all by the hand of Satan. Then, in the final pages of the book, we see how the Lord gave him back even more than he had lost. The text says: "The LORD restored his fortunes. In fact, the LORD gave him twice as much as before! ... The LORD blessed Job in the second half of his life even more than in the beginning" (42:10, 12).

So many passages in the Old Testament speak about how God will one day restore the nation of Israel to its former prominence and glory—and place King Jesus on the throne.

Back in Luke 15, Jesus told a third lost-and-found story, this time about a young man who left his father. He went out and wasted all his inheritance on crazy living, dragging the family name through the gutter. One day, however, he came to his senses and said to himself: *I should just go back. I'll say, "Dad, I know I've completely blown it, and I'm no longer worthy to even be called your son. But maybe you could just give me a job around the ranch. Being your servant would be better than the way I've been living."*

Most of us have heard the story of the prodigal son, but it was brand-new to Jesus' disciples, and I can imagine them hanging on every word—especially as the drama reached its conclusion:

> When he was still a long way off, his father saw
> him. His heart pounding, he ran out, embraced
> him, and kissed him. The son started his speech....
> But the father wasn't listening. He was calling to
> the servants, "Quick. Bring a clean set of clothes

> and dress him. Put the family ring on his finger
> and sandals on his feet.... We're going to feast!
> We're going to have a wonderful time! My son is
> here—given up for dead and now alive! Given up
> for lost and now found!" (Luke 15:20–24 MSG)

Notice this common denominator in the three stories: The lost sheep still belonged to the shepherd. The lost coin was still in the house. And the lost boy was still a son, though a wayward one.

God is the one who restores lost valuables, lost opportunities, lost dreams, and lost relationships.

Can He even restore lost *time*? The apostle Peter reminds us that us that "A day is like a thousand years to the Lord, and a thousand years is like a day" (2 Pet. 3:8). In other words, if He chooses, He can take one day of our lives—even if we have wasted many years—and give it a thousand years' worth of impact.

In the book of Joel, the Lord tells His people:

> So I will restore to you the years that the swarming
>   locust has eaten....
> You shall eat in plenty and be satisfied,
> And praise the name of the LORD your God,
> Who has dealt wondrously with you. (2:25–26 NKJV)

I think about all the future memories our family would have had with our eldest son, Christopher, who died in a tragic automobile accident in 2008.

But he is not just part of our past. He is also part of our future. We know we will see him again and create new memories in Heaven and on the new earth.

God is in the restoration business.

That's our Shepherd. We go astray, we get cast down, but He deals "wondrously" with us. When God's children go sideways, it is in His heart to restore them. And if we know fellow Christians who have left the right path, who've wandered away from the truth, who say they are "deconstructing" their faith, who have backslidden (to use biblical terminology), our objective should be to restore them, not scorn or destroy them.

You don't kick a cast sheep. You don't stand over a cast sheep and shake your finger at it, reminding it how foolish it has been. You don't sit around the campfire with the other shepherds and gossip about that ridiculous sheep on its back, bleating and kicking.

No, of course you don't. You do all you can to help it back to its feet. Again, our objective should always be to restore, not to destroy. That is the heart of the Great Shepherd.

Here's what the book of Galatians tells us:

> Dear brothers, if a Christian is overcome by some sin, you who are godly should gently and humbly help him back onto the right path, remembering that next time it might be one of you who is in the wrong. Share each other's troubles and problems, and so obey our Lord's command. (6:1–2 TLB)

Jude had similar counsel, telling believers, "Be merciful to those who doubt; save others by snatching them from the fire; to others show mercy, mixed with fear" (Jude 22–23 NIV).

Jesus is the Good Shepherd who gives His life for the sheep. David was a shepherd to both sheep and a nation. But we who belong to Jesus are shepherds too. Peter instructs:

> Care for the flock that God has entrusted to you. Watch over it willingly, not grudgingly—not for what you will get out of it, but because you are eager to serve God. Don't lord it over the people assigned to your care, but lead them by your own good example. And when the Great Shepherd appears, you will receive a crown of never-ending glory and honor. (1 Pet. 5:2–4)

I may be a pastor, but every Christian is a shepherd with more influence over our fellow believers than we may ever realize.

Be strong, courageous, merciful, and kind with others.

Shepherd like Jesus.

A PAGE TORN FROM DAVID'S JOURNAL

Why, my soul, are you downcast?
    Why so disturbed within me?
Put your hope in God,
    for I will yet praise him,
    my Savior and my God.

My soul is downcast within me;
    therefore I will remember you
from the land of the Jordan,
    the heights of Hermon—from Mount Mizar.
Deep calls to deep
    in the roar of your waterfalls;
all your waves and breakers
    have swept over me.

By day the LORD directs his love,
    at night his song is with me—
    a prayer to the God of my life.

(Ps. 42:5–8 NIV)

PUT GOD
FIRST

Whom have I in heaven but you?
I desire you more than anything on earth.

Psalm 73:25

Inspired by Psalm 138

David had something big in his mind and heart, and he held on to it through the years.

When did he first begin to dream about building a temple for the God of Israel? Was it after he became king and was settled comfortably in his cedar-paneled palace? Was it while he was fleeing from King Saul, bolting from refuge to refuge in the wilderness? Or was it before that, when he was out under the starry sky, plucking his little harp to soothe his sheep?

It was certainly on his mind when he wrote Psalm 138. In fact, in his mind, the temple was already completed. He wrote:

> I will praise you, LORD, with all my heart;
> before the "gods" I will sing your praise.

> I will bow down toward your holy temple
>   and will praise your name
>   for your unfailing love and your faithfulness.
>   (vv. 1–2 NIV)

Those were good words, but there was one problem. The temple hadn't been built yet. David's son Solomon would finally build the temple after David died. I can't say for sure, but it seems to me that David had been thinking and planning and dreaming about building the Lord a house for a long, long time.

In Psalm 5:7 he told the Lord, "Because of your unfailing love, I can enter your house; I will worship at your Temple with deepest awe." In Psalm 24:3, he spoke about a "holy place" on "the mountain of the LORD."

There was no temple! But David could see it with his heart and in his mind's eye.

So David had that strong priority in life. He wanted to honor God by building Him a magnificent dwelling. God knew all about that desire, and David knew that God knew. He wrote: "You know what I long for, Lord; you hear my every sigh" (Ps. 38:9).

When God had finally given David and Israel peace, David's heartfelt desire came out into the open. Scripture says, "When King David was settled in his palace and the LORD had given him rest from all the surrounding enemies, the king summoned Nathan the prophet. 'Look,' David said, 'I am living in a beautiful cedar palace, but the Ark of God is out there in a tent!'" (2 Sam. 7:1–2).

Honoring God was the overpowering priority in David's life.

The apostle Paul also had a life-shaping priority.

He told the church at Philippi, "I want to know Christ and experience the mighty power that raised him from the dead" (Phil. 3:10). It was his determined purpose and what he desired above all else. It didn't matter if he was stitching tents alongside Priscilla and Aquila, preaching all night in Ephesus, sailing in a storm across the Mediterranean, or languishing in a Roman prison, awaiting execution.

He wanted to know Jesus Christ in an ever-deeper way, and he wanted to give his life to serving the Lord. In that same letter, he told the church, "For to me, to live is Christ" (1:21 NKJV). Sometimes I will hear pastors say, "Man, I'm just burned out in ministry." I don't know what to tell them, because I've been doing it for fifty years and would do it for fifty more if the Lord gave them to me. That's because for me, ministry is not a job—it's a calling.

There have been many times when I have been depleted and physically tired and have found myself energized by preaching or helping someone. There have been times when I have gone to the pulpit at about a 10 percent charge and ended at 100 percent. Why is this? Jesus said:

> Give, and you will receive. Your gift will return to you in full—pressed down, shaken together to make room for more, running over, and poured into your lap. The amount you give will determine the amount you get back. (Luke 6:38)

Yes, at times I get tired *in* the Lord's work, but I never get tired *of* the Lord's work. So I may take a little time off, walk on the beach, hang out with my grandkids, recharge, and then come back thankful for the opportunities before me.

Some people are afraid to completely commit their lives to God or make Him their top priority. They tell themselves, *If I say, "Lord, I'll go where You want me to go and do what You want me to do," something awful will happen to me. He will make me do the worst thing ever. He'll call me to the mission field in some jungle somewhere with poisonous snakes and spiders the size of guinea pigs.*

What a distorted view of God's heart! The truth is, God's plan for you is better than your plan for yourself. The One who created you and knew you in the womb knows where to lead you, place you, use you, and satisfy your deepest desires better than you ever could.

It's an old expression, but I always think of the man who worked hard all his life to "climb the ladder," only to discover near the end of life that the ladder was leaning against the wrong wall.

In Psalm 61:2 David prayed, "When my heart is overwhelmed; lead me to the rock that is higher than I" (NKJV). We all need that higher rock. We need God's perspective on our lives. He has a higher, better, more-fulfilling purpose for us than we could ever cobble together on our own.

At the end of his life, when it came time to hand off the kingdom to Solomon, David gave this counsel: "Solomon my son, know the God of your father and serve him with a whole heart and with a willing mind" (1 Chron. 28:9 ESV).

In later days, Solomon would look back and reflect on how his dad had made the Lord his highest priority. David had been a good example. Not a perfect one, by any means, but he left a straight path for his boy to follow.

David had longed to build a temple for the God of Israel, and Solomon built it.

Could you say this to your son or daughter or grandchild: "Serve the Lord like I have served the Lord; live for Jesus as I have sought to live for Jesus"?

In 1 Corinthians 11:1, Paul said, "Follow my example, as I follow the example of Christ" (NIV). In other words, put God first in your life, and everything else will find its proper balance. Put your relationship with Jesus first in your life, and others will take note of it. Your children and grandchildren will think about it as they make their own choices and choose their own paths.

Jesus said, "Seek the Kingdom of God above all else, and live righteously, and he will give you everything you need" (Matt. 6:33).

Before that, He said, "Don't be like nonbelievers, because all they think about is what they're going to eat, what they're going to drink, and what they're going to wear" (see vv. 31–32). And we might add "what they're going to drive, where they're going to live, and how their careers will advance."

Jesus says, "Seek God's kingdom first. Make it number one." Yes, you will still think about what you will wear, what you will have for lunch, and what you will do on the weekend. You will still spend time pondering a career path.

He is telling us to think more about God's rule and reign in our lives than those other things—and to give Him priority in all our thoughts and plans.

Solomon had his first test not long after becoming king. The Lord came to him one night in a dream and said, "Ask for whatever you want me to give you" (1 Kings 3:5 NIV).

Can you imagine that? What if God appeared to you tonight and offered you the very same thing. "What can I give you? Ask" (MSG).

I was telling this story to two of my granddaughters, Stella and Lucy, the other night. I asked Lucy, "What would you do if God did that for you? What would you ask for?"

She said, "I would order a chocolate lava crunch cake from Domino's." (I don't even know what that is.) When it comes to sugar, Lucy is a heat-seeking missile. If there is a cookie hidden somewhere in the house, she will find it.

What would *you* ask for? A house? A car? A relationship? A massive pile of money?

Solomon didn't hesitate. He asked the Lord for wisdom to rule God's people—which was a great answer and one that pleased the Lord. But listen to how he began his reply:

> You showed great and faithful love to your servant my father, David, because he was honest and true and faithful to you. And you have continued to show this great and faithful love to him today by giving him a son to sit on his throne. (1 Kings 3:6)

He was saying, "Lord, You blessed my father because he walked with You. And now I need that blessing in my life too. Help me to be like Dad."

Obviously, Solomon—the son of David and Bathsheba—knew all about his father's great failures and sins. But when it came time to make some big choices, the thing he remembered most was

David's burning desire to honor God. What he remembered was that his father had been "honest and true and faithful" to the God of Israel.

When you put God first, people around you will take note, even if they don't say anything. Like a rock tossed into a still pond, your decision to put God first will send out ripples that will touch future generations, long after you have left the planet.

Do you doubt it? You're reading a book about someone who made God his highest priority—three thousand years ago.

A Page Torn from David's Journal

I give you thanks, O LORD, with all my heart;
  I will sing your praises before the gods.
I bow before your holy Temple as I worship.
  I praise your name for your unfailing love and
      faithfulness;
for your promises are backed
  by all the honor of your name.
As soon as I pray, you answer me;
  you encourage me by giving me strength....

Though I am surrounded by troubles,
  you will protect me from the anger of my enemies.
You reach out your hand,
  and the power of your right hand saves me.

The LORD will work out his plans for my life—
   for your faithful love, O LORD, endures forever.
Don't abandon me, for you made me.

(Ps. 138:1–3, 7–8)

RESTING IN THE ETERNAL GOD

My days vanish like smoke...,
like the evening shadow.

Psalm 102:3, 11 (NIV)

Inspired by Psalms 90 and 102

No one knows for sure who wrote Psalm 102.

Whoever it was, he really wanted people to read it.

In fact, he wanted you and me to read it. This is the only psalm where the writer actually gave instructions for what he wanted done with it. He wrote: "Let this be recorded for future generations" (v. 18).

It reminds me of a country-and-western song by George Strait, "Write This Down." The author wanted his words to have an impact after he was gone.

And they have! Here we are reading Psalm 102 all these centuries later. *We* are the future generation he was writing to. So what did he want to get across to us?

In many ways, the psalm starts out like a gut punch. The writer is *very* distressed. The needle on his stress gauge is bouncing way up in the red zone. In our Bibles, we read the title: "A prayer of one overwhelmed with trouble, pouring out problems before the LORD." In other words, this guy was near the end of his rope.

Some Bible scholars think this sounds like David. They say he might have written it during the time he was fleeing from his son Absalom, and that would make sense. His own son was trying to kill him and had forced him to leave his throne and palace and escape into the wilderness with nothing more than the clothes on his back. He would definitely be torn, because Absalom, as wickedly as he was behaving, was still David's son, whom he loved. But he also was his enemy, wanting him dead.

The worst kind of betrayal we can experience is from a member of our family, especially one of our children.

Of all the low moments in David's life, this must have been among the lowest. He was probably sixty years old at the time, and it looked as though he had lost everything.

The writer of Psalm 102 was looking back on his life and thinking about how quickly it had passed. Even as he wrote this psalm, he seemed to feel time slipping through his fingers:

> LORD, hear my prayer!
>   Listen to my plea!
> Don't turn away from me
>   in my time of distress.

Bend down to listen,
  and answer me quickly when I call to you.
For my days disappear like smoke. (vv. 1–3)

We can imagine David lying on his torn royal robe, soaked with tears, at night in the wilderness, feeling lonely and desolate.

I am like an owl in the desert,
  like a little owl in a far-off wilderness.
I lie awake,
  lonely as a solitary bird on the roof.
My enemies taunt me day after day.
  They mock and curse me. (vv. 6–8)

It was bad enough to be chased by the Philistines or hounded and hated by Saul. But this was his own son! Again, he feels like his life is slipping away from him: "My life passes as swiftly as the evening shadows. I am withering away like grass.... He broke my strength in midlife, cutting short my days" (vv. 11, 23).

Moses reflected on the same theme in Psalm 90.

Seventy years are given to us!
  Some even live to eighty.
But even the best years are filled with pain and trouble;
  soon they disappear, and we fly away. (v. 10)

Thinking about the brevity of life could be a depressing thought. But right in the middle of these thoughts, Moses gives us this golden nugget of wisdom: "So teach us to number our days, that we may gain a heart of wisdom" (v. 12 NKJV). Another version puts it like this: "Teach us to number our days and recognize how few they are; help us to spend them as we should" (TLB).

Life is filled with opportunities, but the big question is, What do we do with them? Do we let them slip by, saying, "Maybe next time. There's always another day"? Or do we seize them?

We may not have as much time as we think.

In Ephesians 5:15–17, Paul wrote: "Be very careful, then, how you live—not as unwise but as wise, making the most of every opportunity, because the days are evil. Therefore do not be foolish, but understand what the Lord's will is" (NIV).

God has given us each a certain number of days to walk on this planet. None of us knows how many days that is. But the Bible urges us to use them wisely.

Leslie Weatherhead, an English pastor and writer, calculated the average length of a life using the hours of one day to illustrate the importance of recognizing the value of time. He concluded that if you are fifteen years old, the time is 10:25 a.m. If your age is twenty, the time is 11:34 a.m. If you're thirty, the time is 1:51 p.m. If you're forty, the time is 4:08 p.m. If you're fifty, the time is 6:25 p.m. If you're sixty, the time is 8:42 p.m. And if you're seventy, the time is 11:00 p.m.

In Luke 19, Jesus told the story of a man who went on a journey and left some money with his servants to use while he was away. This was not an uncommon thing in those days. A wealthy man or a ruler would have many servants in his household, from those who performed basic labor to those who managed the financial affairs of his household, even his business. In many cases, some of the man's servants would be better educated and more skilled than he was. Highly trusted servants virtually had a free hand within prescribed areas of responsibility while the owner was home.

When the owner would go on a journey, he would leave full authority in the hands of these key servants, who would have the ancient equivalent of a power of attorney. So Jesus described a scenario in which a wealthy man went on a journey and left the key servants in charge of his possessions. It's difficult to know exactly what sum he left them, but one possibility is he gave the equivalent of $5,000 to the first servant, $2,000 to the second servant, and $1,000 to the third.

What is Jesus' story saying to us? I think it's obvious. Jesus is like that wealthy man who goes on a journey, which spans the day He left this earth to the day He will return in the Second Coming. We are the servants He has invested in, and we are to take what He has given us and use it for His glory while we await His return.

Christ has paid an incalculable debt for us. He has pardoned us. He has forgiven us. And now we should become His servants, not because we have to but because we want to—because we love Him. We recognize that He has instilled certain things in our lives that we are to use for His glory. Certain gifts. Certain talents. Certain resources. Unique opportunities. Everything. God has given to each of us three valuable commodities: time, talent, and treasure.

We need to invest them all wisely.

If we will humble ourselves before Him, if we take what we have and offer it to God, if we are willing to do what He has placed before us to do and to be faithful in the little things, then He will give us more to do. I would rather try and fail than never try at all. Anytime you take a chance, you can fail. But it's better to try than to never take chances and never have anything happen in your life.

So seize the day. Seize the moment. Seize the opportunities before you. Step out of your comfort zone for His sake.

Don't put it off too long either, because as I have said before, you may not have as much time as you think. Be productive with your life. Be productive with your time. Reach out and grasp the opportunities God has given you.

In 1 Corinthians 15:58, we read these encouraging words:

> My dear brothers, since future victory is sure, be strong and steady, always abounding in the Lord's work, for you know that nothing you do for the Lord is ever wasted. (TLB)

Back in Psalm 102, the psalmist—perhaps David—makes a transition from thinking about the shortness of his life to the eternal life of God. When the fog of his discouragement clears in the night, he sees the vast, starry heavens and writes:

> You, O LORD, will sit on your throne forever.
>   Your fame will endure to every generation....
>
> You are always the same;
>   you will live forever.
> The children of your people
>   will live in security.

Their children's children
    will thrive in your presence. (vv. 12, 27–28)

As creatures of earth, our time here is very limited. But as sons and daughters of the living God, an eternity in Heaven with Him awaits us. We need the guidance of the Holy Spirit to "number our days" and make the most of each one (Ps. 90:12 NKJV).

A PAGE TORN FROM DAVID'S JOURNAL

He will listen to the prayers of the destitute, for he is never too busy to heed their requests. I am recording this so that future generations will also praise the Lord for all that he has done. And a people that shall be created shall praise the Lord....

In ages past you laid the foundations of the earth and made the heavens with your hands! They shall perish, but you go on forever. They will grow old like worn-out clothing, and you will change them like a man putting on a new shirt and throwing away the old one! But you yourself never grow old. You are forever, and your years never end.

But our families will continue; generation after generation will be preserved by your protection.

(Ps. 102:17–18, 25–28 TLB)

Don't Make
Deals with
the Devil

*I cry out to God Most High,
to God who fulfills his purpose for me.*
Psalm 57:2 (ESV)

Inspired by 1 Samuel 24; Psalm 57

I have a friend who is a master negotiator. If I ever want to purchase something bigger than a toothbrush, I ask Steve to do it for me. I call him "the force of nature," because getting good deals is second nature to him, and he is so effective.

But don't *buy* anything from him. Don't personally negotiate with a master negotiator, because no matter what, he always comes out on top.

My friend is a godly man. But you might say the Devil is a master negotiator. In reality, though, he is a master *manipulator*. Any deal you enter into with him will be a losing deal for you. That's why the Bible tells us in Ephesians 4:27 not to "give place to the devil" (NKJV).

Another translation puts it this way: "Do not give the devil a foothold" (NIV).

The dictionary definition of *foothold* tells you all you need to know about Satan's strategy in your life. A foothold, it says, is "a position usable as a base for further advance."[1]

If a rock climber gains a foothold while scaling a rocky cliff, he's not going to stay there and have tea. He's going to keep reaching and crawling along, finding new footholds, until he finally conquers the precipice.

Satan is evil and extremely cunning, and he has been honing his craft for a long, long time. The apostle Paul spoke about the Devil "outsmart[ing]" Christians and said "we are familiar with his evil schemes" (2 Cor. 2:11). Satan knows he probably won't bring down a believer in one fell swoop—in one brazen frontal attack. Instead, he seeks to dismantle us a little at a time through the subtle strategy of compromise.

Show me a Christian who has started to compromise in their life, and I will show you a Christian headed toward spiritual ruin.

For much of David's young life, he was on the run from Saul. I really can't imagine what it would be like to be a fugitive, always looking over your shoulder, always searching for hiding places. I'm reminded of a line from the song "Secret Agent Man" by Johnny Rivers that says the odds were good that the secret agent wouldn't live to see tomorrow.

David was especially upset in 1 Samuel 22 because one of Saul's spies had just ratted on David for visiting Ahimelech the priest in the little town of Nob. As a result, Saul's goons killed the priest and his family and wiped out the little town.

So where could David flee? Where could he go? His family had effectively abandoned him, his wife had betrayed him, his best friend couldn't help him, and his father-in-law wanted his head.

This would have been a great time to seek the Lord's counsel, but Scripture doesn't say that David did that. Instead, he fled to Gath, to the Philistine king, for protection. Was it a lapse of faith? Possibly. It certainly seemed like he was attempting to take matters into his own hands, and that never works out well. And it didn't this time either. He ended up running from Gath, still in fear for his life.

Sometimes people in a situation like this begin to entertain thoughts of suicide. They may say to themselves, *Maybe it would be better if I weren't even here. Maybe if I just left this world, the pain would end.* What they don't realize is that the pain would just begin for those left behind.

Don't let the Devil whisper in your ear. Don't let him tell you that you are unwanted or unloved or that there's no way out of the corner you're in. No matter what your situation, you are loved and wanted by God Himself, and if the truth were known, you are loved and needed by more people than you realize.

After the low point in Gath, however, David's situation began to change. In fact, after David headed to the cave of Adullam, he was soon joined by a ragtag group of rebels and rugged adventurers who were as opposed to Saul as he was.

> Soon his brothers and all his other relatives joined him there. Then others began coming—men who were in trouble or in debt or who were just

> discontented—until David was the captain of
> about 400 men. (1 Sam. 22:1–2)

That must have been encouraging—especially to see his brothers finally rally around him. One minute you're alone, and the next you're the captain of a little army.

This was the context for Psalm 57. This was when David began praising the Lord again and seeking God's face. Maybe the son of Jesse taught his little army around the campfire the new song he had just written:

> Be exalted, O God, above the heavens;
> Let Your glory be above all the earth....
> My heart is steadfast, O God, my heart is
>   steadfast;
> I will sing and give praise.
> Awake, my glory!
> Awake, lute and harp!
> I will awaken the dawn. (vv. 5, 7–8 NKJV)

It must have been an encouraging moment for sure, but what David didn't realize was that Satan was setting him up for one of the biggest tests he would ever face. It would appear to be a great opportunity. But in reality, it was a potential trap.

On his way back home after a battle with the Philistines, Saul stopped at a random cave to answer the call of nature, as they say. But it just so happened that David and his men were hiding in the back of that same cave.

Here's how it went down:

> "Now's your opportunity!" David's men whispered
> to him. "Today the LORD is telling you, 'I will cer-
> tainly put your enemy into your power, to do with
> as you wish.'" So David crept forward and cut off a
> piece of the hem of Saul's robe.
>
> But then David's conscience began bothering
> him because he had cut Saul's robe. He said to his
> men, "The LORD forbid that I should do this to
> my lord the king. I shouldn't attack the LORD's
> anointed one, for the LORD himself has chosen
> him." So David restrained his men and did not let
> them kill Saul. (1 Sam. 24:4–7)

What an interesting twist in the story! It looked for all the world like God had delivered David's enemy into his hands. Here was the wild-eyed tyrant who had ruined David's marriage and reputation. Here was the very man who had been chasing David from one end of the land to the other, trying to kill him. Even David's parents weren't safe from Saul. He had to send them off to a neighboring king for protection.

David's men were saying, "Oh, yeah, this is the Lord's doing, for sure. No way is this random! The Lord Himself dropped this into your lap. So go for it. Do it now! Slit his throat with your knife!"

Essentially, Satan was offering David a shortcut. This is one of his most well-worn strategies. Instead of waiting for the Lord—the Lord's will, the Lord's way, and the Lord's timing—Satan whispers, "You can have it all right now! It's yours! Take it!"

It's what he whispers to the young adult who gets tired of waiting for a Christian to date and fall in love with. He tempts that person to say, "Man, I can't find anybody. It's not working out. I'll just go out with this non-Christian who is interested in me. Maybe I can win this person to the Lord." It's what Satan says to the young couple who want to sleep together right away instead of following God's plan and waiting for marriage. It's what he offers the student who finds a way to cheat on an important exam instead of hitting the books and learning the material.

In fact, it is what the Devil offered Jesus in the wilderness. We read in the gospel of Matthew:

> The Devil took him to the peak of a huge mountain. He gestured expansively, pointing out all the earth's kingdoms, how glorious they all were. Then he said, "They're yours—lock, stock, and barrel. Just go down on your knees and worship me, and they're yours." (4:8–9 MSG)

It was a shortcut. Satan knew that Jesus would one day rule the nations (the Devil knows his Bible very well), but he asked Jesus, "Why go through suffering? Why endure the humiliation and the cross?"

Thank the Lord, Jesus rejected that shortcut. He knew the path before Him, and He was willing to wait for His Father's timing. And "for the joy that was set before Him endured the cross, despising the shame, and ... sat down at the right hand of the throne of God" (Heb. 12:2 NKJV).

David passed the test too. Instead of stabbing his enemy to death, he used his sharp knife to cut a corner off the king's robe. But even that bothered him. No matter what, he would not raise his hand against the man the Lord had anointed to lead Israel. If David was ever going to be king, it would be in God's way and in God's time.

That's true for us as well. We need to do God's will in the right way at the right time. We need to trust and believe that God will accomplish His will for us in His time.

That means closing our ears to Satan's offer of a shortcut.

Don't give him any room to negotiate with you. You will never win anything from him but grief and loss.

A Page Torn from David's Journal

Have mercy on me, O God, have mercy!
 I look to you for protection.
I will hide beneath the shadow of your wings
 until the danger passes by.
I cry out to God Most High,
 to God who will fulfill his purpose for me.
He will send help from heaven to rescue me,
 disgracing those who hound me.
My God will send forth his unfailing love and
 faithfulness....

I will thank you, Lord, among all the people.
 I will sing your praises among the nations.

For your unfailing love is as high as the heavens.
Your faithfulness reaches to the clouds.

Be exalted, O God, above the highest heavens.
May your glory shine over all the earth.

(Ps. 57:1–3, 9–11)

THE LORD'S ARMY

He lifts the poor from the dust
and the needy from the garbage dump.
He sets them among princes.

Psalm 113:7–8

Inspired by 1 Samuel 22; Psalm 18

So who showed up at the cave of Adullam to join David's army? Why did they come, and who got the word out?

In the old days, the US Army would put up posters around the country featuring a stern-faced Uncle Sam pointing a forefinger and saying, "I Want YOU for U.S. Army."

The poster originated in 1917, when World War I was raging in Europe. America's political leadership must have seen the handwriting on the wall and knew that our country needed to beef up its armed forces. So they commissioned an artist to come up with the iconic picture of Uncle Sam and the words "I want YOU."

It worked. The impact of the poster was felt across the country, and young men and women responded to this call to duty. It was more than just a call to arms—it was a rallying cry for patriotic citizens to step up.

In the 1970s someone came up with a little friendlier slogan. Ads on TV proclaimed, "Today's Army wants to join you!"

The 1980s Army had a TV ad of happy-looking men and women jumping out of helicopters or scaling walls with the catchy little jingle: "Be all you can be ... in the Army."

What kind of recruiting campaign did David have to gather four hundred men out in the wilderness?

Well, of course, there was no campaign at all. There were no posters, handbills, or commercials. David didn't even know the men were coming. They just showed up. *The Message* version captures that unique moment well:

> David got away and escaped to the Cave of Adullam. When his brothers and others associated with his family heard where he was, they came down and joined him. Not only that, but all who were down on their luck came around—losers and vagrants and misfits of all sorts. David became their leader. There were about four hundred in all. (1 Sam. 22:1–2)

Recruiting posters wouldn't have worked anyway. Saul's men would have torn them down. And can you imagine a picture of a bunch of guys in dirty clothes and bristly beards pictured over the slogan "Be all you can be"?

So where did they come from? How did they know about David and the cave? Was it the Lord who gathered them to fight with

David? Maybe so. But what a motley crew this was—and I don't mean the rock group.

Some translations say these guys were 3D—*distressed*, in *debt*, and *discontented* (see NIV, NKJV).

No one observing them at the mouth of that cave would have called them Israel's elite soldiers. In fact, they were stressed out, uptight, and bitter of soul. They felt themselves mistreated by the world, and they weren't happy about it. Honestly, are these the kind of people you'd even like to go get coffee with? Is this the army you'd want at your back?

Nevertheless, this was David's new team.

And out of this group of unhappy misfits God was going to bring a mighty army. A number of them would later be known as David's "mighty men of valor" (1 Chron. 12:21 ESV). Their unbelievable exploits still leave us stunned to this day, and they would rule with David when he finally ascended the throne.

Here's the point: *God specializes in taking the outcasts of this culture and turning them into men and women of God.*

Think about the apostles. For two thousand years we have put these guys on pedestals. They have been carved into statues and their likenesses worked into beautiful stained-glass windows two stories high. And they did become powerful, Spirit-filled men in the Lord's service. But when Jesus chose them, they were just like you and me. They were normal people with all kinds of quirks.

Peter was impulsive and hotheaded, prone to speaking first and thinking later. And James and John? The Lord didn't call them "the Sons of Thunder" for nothing (Mark 3:17). On one occasion, they wanted to call fire down from Heaven on a city that hadn't shown them hospitality. Then there was Matthew, the tax collector, up to his eyeballs in collaboration with Israel's Roman overlords. His fellow Jews considered him a traitor.

Simon the Zealot might has well have been called "Simon the Terrorist." He had dedicated himself to the violent overthrow of Rome, and he wasn't picky about his methods. And we know about Thomas, who seemed to struggle with doubt right up to the end.

Later, Jesus would draft Saul, who became Paul, into His army. This was the man who hated Christians, forcibly shut down churches, and had godly men and women dragged away from their families and executed. He also played a role in seeing the godly young man Stephen put to death.

Jesus Himself handpicked these guys, transformed them into apostles, and turned the world upside down with them. It was that same apostle Paul who wrote to the Corinthians: "Isn't it obvious that God deliberately chose men and women that the culture overlooks and exploits and abuses, chose these 'nobodies' to expose the hollow pretensions of the 'somebodies'?" (1 Cor. 1:27–28 MSG).

Think about your own life before you turned to the Lord. I think about mine, and I can tell you, it's not like God got some great prize when the seventeen-year-old Greg Laurie believed in Jesus. I was just a mixed-up kid who mocked the Christians on my high school campus and was definitely headed in the wrong direction in life.

Back at the cave, God had assembled a band of unlikely rejects and ne'er-do-wells to form David's army. Against all odds, they would take on the establishment and the enemies of the Lord.

As I have mentioned, David wrote Psalm 57 during this time, and it makes you think he might not have been completely comfortable with his new "friends." He wrote: "My soul is among lions; I lie among the sons of men who are set on fire, whose teeth are spears and arrows, and their tongue a sharp sword" (Ps. 57:4 NJKV). This wasn't like a Boy Scout troop. It might have been more like camping out with Hells Angels.

But David saw them for who they would become.

And did you know that God sees you the same way? What do you see when you look in a mirror—or maybe even a magnifying mirror? (Those are no fun at all.) Most likely, you see all your flaws, blemishes, and shortcomings. But God sees you differently than how you see yourself. I said something like this on day 5:

> We see a blank canvas. God sees a finished painting.
> We see failure. God sees potential.
> We see a mess. God sees a message.
> We see a zero. God sees a potential hero.

And David's scruffy rabble of dropouts and outlaws would become mighty men of God. How mighty? It's hard to even wrap our minds around what they accomplished in the days and years to come. Jashobeam the Hacmonite, for instance, "once used his spear to kill 300 enemy warriors in a single battle" (1 Chron. 11:11). Then there was Eleazar, son of Dodai, who stood back-to-back with David in a barley field fighting a troop of Philistines, and God gave them victory (see vv. 12–14). (Talk about someone "having your back"!) And there was Benaiah, who "also went down into a pit on a snowy day and killed a lion" (2 Sam. 23:20 NIV).

These men may have come from underprivileged, unhappy backgrounds. But it didn't matter to the Lord (or to David). None of them were disqualified by their past.

It's the same for us.

God can and will use you if you surrender completely to Him and stay obedient and available. I like the way Paul described it to the Corinthian believers. Speaking about the life of Christ within us, he said, "This priceless treasure we hold, so to speak, in a common earthenware jar—to show that the splendid power of it belongs to God and not to us" (2 Cor. 4:7 PHILLIPS).

I love that. We are ordinary jars that He fills with His treasure, His life.

Don't let Satan (or anyone else) make you feel disqualified for that honor. It doesn't matter if you're reading this in a prison cell or a rehab center. It doesn't matter what your track record has been. It doesn't matter if other people have minimized you, ignored you, or rejected you.

The Son of David wants you for one of His mighty men and mighty women in these perilous days before He returns.

What a privilege!

My son Jonathan told me the story about when his older brother, Christopher, took him to a rather unusual church on a Sunday morning. It was filled with a bunch of people who had come out of rehab and prison. The greeter at the front door had an eye patch and skull and crossbones tatted on his forehead! Jonathan had put on a clean shirt that day, and he immediately began to judge these people by their outward appearance.

But when the worship service began and he saw the passion and devotion they had for God, he realized that they were pleasing to the Lord and he was not. He was compromising in his spiritual life at that point, and his brother taught him a valuable lesson: don't judge a book by its cover.

Remember again the story of when the prophet Samuel came to the house of Jesse looking for the next king of Israel after God had rejected King Saul.

As Samuel found himself impressed in particular with David's oldest brother, Eliab, who stood taller than the others, the Lord said, "Don't judge by his appearance or height, for I have rejected him. The LORD doesn't see things the way you see them. People judge by outward appearance, but the LORD looks at the heart" (1 Sam. 16:7).

Be careful about making a snap judgment about anyone. The person you minimize or undervalue today may be the one who tomorrow takes on a lion in a snowy pit for the name of Jesus.

A Page Torn from David's Journal

> God arms me with strength,
>   and he makes my way perfect.
> He makes me as surefooted as a deer,
>   enabling me to stand on mountain heights.
> He trains my hands for battle;
>   he strengthens my arm to draw a bronze bow.

You have given me your shield of victory.
    Your right hand supports me;
    your help has made me great.
You have made a wide path for my feet
    to keep them from slipping....

The LORD lives! Praise to my Rock!
    May the God of my salvation be exalted!
He is the God who pays back those who harm me;
    he subdues the nations under me
    and rescues me from my enemies.
You hold me safe beyond the reach of my enemies;
    you save me from violent opponents.
For this, O LORD, I will praise you among the
            nations;
    I will sing praises to your name.
You give great victories to your king;
    you show unfailing love to your anointed,
    to David and all his descendants forever.

(Ps. 18:32–36, 46–50)

THE ROAD MAP

Two centuries after David's death, Israel had sunk about as low as it had ever been. The nation had already seen plenty of dark days. But had it ever been this dark?

Maybe not.

The country had been torn in two since the days of Solomon's son Rehoboam. The northern kingdom, Israel, had turned away from the Lord completely. Only the tribe of Judah and the little tribe of Benjamin remained faithful to the God of Abraham. And then, with the coming of King Ahaz, all that changed.

He led the nation in turning away from the Lord to the worship of idols. He actually sacrificed his own sons in the fire to foreign gods. Not satisfied with that, he emptied the Lord's temple of its furnishings and boarded up the doors. He set up idols on literally every street corner in Jerusalem. Grotesque, false gods were as common as traffic lights in Los Angeles.

As you might expect, the results of this idolatry were crushing military defeats, humiliation, death, and sorrow.

Finally, a new king took the throne. His name was Hezekiah.

The new king—the new sheriff in town—loved the Lord and began cleaning house on day one. But after the nation had fallen so far, failed so horribly, and rebelled so completely against the Lord, how could even a good king and a lost nation find the way back?

As it turned out, Hezekiah found an old road map. One that had belonged to King David.

After Hezekiah trashed the demonic idols and power-washed Jerusalem, the Bible says:

> King Hezekiah then stationed the Levites at the Temple of the LORD with cymbals, lyres, and harps. He obeyed all the commands that the LORD had given to King David.... The Levites then took their positions around the Temple with the instruments of David, and the priests took their positions with the trumpets....
>
> As the burnt offering was presented, songs of praise to the LORD were begun, accompanied by the trumpets and other instruments of David, the former king of Israel.... Then the king and everyone with him bowed down in worship. King Hezekiah and the officials ordered the Levites to praise the LORD with the psalms written by David and by Asaph the seer. So they offered joyous praise and bowed down in worship. (2 Chron. 29:25–27, 29–30)

They followed David's map. They obeyed David's instructions. They played David's instruments. They sang David's psalms.

And joy washed over God's people like a flood.

The psalms, those old songs of praise and repentance and delight in the Lord that had been collecting dust in moldering boxes in the temple basement, were brought out into the sunlight. People brushed off the dust, and the psalms were as good as ever. Or maybe even better.

People from all over the broken nation, north and south, began filtering back to Jerusalem.

They offered sacrifices, they prayed, they feasted, they sang, they worshipped the God of their fathers, and the crowds just kept on growing.

The Bible says, "There was great joy in the city, for Jerusalem had not seen a celebration like this one since the days of Solomon, King David's son. Then the priests and Levites stood and blessed the people, and God heard their prayer from his holy dwelling in heaven" (2 Chron. 30:26–27).

And here we are, three thousand years later, in a nation that honored and worshipped the Lord at its founding but seems to have mostly lost its way. We need to find our way back too. We need a road map, a spiritual GPS, to help us return to the God we have neglected, ignored, sometimes mocked, and largely forgotten.

But it really isn't that complicated.

We already have the road map. Jesus, the Son of David, of the ancient line of the house of David, our Lord and Shepherd and Savior, said, "I am the Way" (John 14:6).

And like every return journey, the way back home begins with a first step.

Toward Him.

— NOTES —

Day 1

1. C. H. Spurgeon, "Psalm 23," Blue Letter Bible, accessed July 22, 2024, www.blueletterbible.org/Comm/spurgeon_charles/tod/ps023.cfm.

Day 2

1. "How Intelligent Are Dolphins?," WDC, accessed July 29, 2024, https://us.whales.org/whales-dolphins/how-intelligent-are-dolphins.

2. "Can Cats Find Their Way Home from Miles Away?," *Cat Bandit* (blog), accessed August 8, 2024, https://blog.catbandit.com/can-cats-find-their-way-home-from-miles-away.

3. Tim Challies, "Dumb, Directionless, Defenseless," *Challies* (blog), August 26, 2013, www.challies.com/christian-living/dumb-directionless-defenseless.

4. Challies, "Dumb, Directionless, Defenseless."

Day 5

1. George Herbert, *A Priest to the Temple; or, The Country Parson, His Character and Rule of Holy Life* (London: N.p., 1652), chap. 7, https://ccel.org/ccel/herbert/temple2/temple2.x.html.

2. "Americans Spent More than $16.5 Billion on Cosmetic Plastic Surgery in 2018," American Society of Plastic Surgeons, April 10, 2019, www.plasticsurgery

.org/news/press-releases/americans-spent-more-than-16-billion-on-cosmetic
-plastic-surgery-in-2018.

3. "Scholarly Analysis of the Kennedy-Nixon Debates," Purdue University,
accessed October 15, 2024, https://cla.purdue.edu/academic/history/debate
/kennedynixon/kennedynixonscholarly.html.

4. Alan Slater et al., "Newborn Infants' Preference for Attractive Faces: The Role
of Internal and External Facial Features," *Infancy* 1, no. 2 (2000): 265–74,
www.babylab.ucla.edu/wp-content/uploads/sites/8/2016/09/Slater-et-al
-2000.pdf.

Day 10

1. See Eugene Peterson, *A Long Obedience in the Same Direction: Discipleship in an
Instant Society*, (Downer's Grove, IL: IVP Books, 2000), 202.

Day 11

1. Charles Spurgeon, "The Truly Blessed Man," Spurgeon's Sermons, Christian
Classics Ethereal Library, accessed July 22, 2024, https://ccel.org/ccel/spurgeon
/sermons57/sermons57.xl.html.

2. Robert Frost, "The Road Not Taken," Poetry Foundation, accessed July 22,
2024, www.poetryfoundation.org/poems/44272/the-road-not-taken.

Day 12

1. Guy Faulconbridge, "How Many Nuclear Weapons Does Russia Have and Who
Controls Them?," Reuters, September 27, 2024, www.reuters.com/world/europe
/russias-nuclear-arsenal-how-big-is-it-who-controls-it-2024-03-13.

Day 14

1. Stephen Covey, *The 7 Habits of Highly Effective People* (New York: Simon &
Schuster, 2020).

Day 15

1. C. S. Lewis, *The Problem of Pain*, in *The Complete C. S. Lewis Signature Classics* (New York: HarperOne, 2002), 604.

2. Greg Laurie, interview by Larry King, *Larry King Live*, CNN, August 4, 2005.

Day 16

1. See Eugene Peterson, *A Long Obedience in the Same Direction: Discipleship in an Instant Society*, (Downer's Grove, IL: IVP Books, 2000), 202.

Day 20

1. Josh Tyrangiel, "A New AI Predicts When We'll Die. It Says Even More about How We Live," *Washington Post*, January 15, 2024, www.washingtonpost.com /opinions/2024/01/15/artificial-intelligence-death-calculator.

2. Marco della Cava, "With Project Blueprint, Tech Millionaire Bryan Johnson Is Trying to Be 18 Again. Literally," *USA Today*, January 27, 2023, www.usatoday.com/story/life/health-wellness/2023/01/27/want-feel-18-again -tech-ceo-spending-2-million/11133790002; Eleanor Pringle, "Bryan Johnson, the Tech Founder Spending Millions to Be 18 Again, Says His Goal Is to Make Death Optional," Fortune Well, February 17, 2024, https://fortune.com /well/2024/02/17/bryan-johnson-blueprint-protocol-aim-death-optional.

3. Scott Stump, "'It's Got to Be Crispy': Woman, 105, Says Bacon Key to Longevity," *Today*, March 8, 2013, www.today.com/food/its-got-be-crispy -woman-105-says-bacon-key-longevity-1c9846050.

4. Yvette Alt Miller, "Dovid, Melech Yisrael: 4 Facts about This Iconic Jewish Song," Aish, accessed July 30, 2024, https://aish.com/dovid-melech-yisrael -4-facts-about-this-iconic-jewish-song.

Day 21

1. Max Lucado, *A Love Worth Giving* (Nashville, TN: Thomas Nelson, 2002), 104.

Day 22

1. Corrie ten Boom, *God Is My Hiding Place: 40 Devotions for Refuge and Strength* (Minneapolis, MN: Chosen, 2021).

Day 24

1. C. S. Lewis, *Letters to Malcolm: Chiefly on Prayer* (London: Geoffrey Bles, 1964), Letter 14, www.gutenberg.ca/ebooks/lewiscs-letterstomalcolm /lewiscs-letterstomalcolm-00-h.html.

Day 26

1. W. Phillip Keller, *A Shepherd Looks at Psalm 23* (Grand Rapids, MI: Zondervan, 2007), 70.

2. Marija Bern, "50 Unbelievable Stories of People Finding Things They Thought They Lost Forever," Bored Panda, August 23, 2017, www.boredpanda.com/lost-found-items.

Day 29

1. *Merriam-Webster*, s.v. "foothold," accessed July 30, 2024, www.merriam-webster.com/dictionary/foothold.

DAVID C COOK

JOIN US.
SPREAD THE GOSPEL.
CHANGE THE WORLD.

We believe in equipping the local church with Christ-centered resources that empower believers, even in the most challenging places on earth.

We trust that God is *always* at work, in the power of Jesus and the presence of the Holy Spirit, inviting people into relationship with Him.

We are committed to spreading the gospel throughout the world— across villages, cities, and nations. We trust that the Word of God will transform lives and communities by bringing light to the darkness.

As a global ministry with a 150-year legacy, David C Cook is dedicated to this mission. Each time you purchase a resource or donate, you're supporting a ministry—helping spread the gospel, disciple believers, and raise up leaders in some of the world's most underserved regions.

Your support fuels this mission.
Your partnership sends the gospel where it's needed most.

Discover more. Be the difference.
Visit DavidCCook.org/Donate